A Deepening Life

Joan Grundy

To St. Joseph's,

May something here deepen your life,

Joan Grundy

Printed in Canada

ISBN 978-0-9947511-0-2

Kayak front cover image: Joan Grundy

FIN 18 05 2016

Library and Archives Canada Cataloguing in Publication

Grundy, Joan, 1961-, author
A deepening life / Joan Grundy.

ISBN 978-0-9947511-0-2 (paperback)

I. Title.

PS8613.R86D44 2015 C813'.6 C2015-903567-8

For my parents, Jean and Fred Grundy
In abiding gratitude for loving me into being

At its essence the soul longs to be whole and free. In mid-life I felt the tug of my soul calling me to deeper integration and fullness of spirit. Writing this book has been an essential response to this invitation. Often in life, I tried to go up and over, but I followed the call to go down and deeper… and it has made all the difference.

Contents

I have carried the idea of writing this book in my heart for a prolonged period of time, yet struggled for more than a decade to get down to the task of writing it. Was this simply procrastination on my part, or was something deeper at work? A number of years back, as I was berating myself for not yet having started to write, a good friend suggested that my book would be written when it was meant to be written, and that my words would contain greater wisdom for the "seasoning." I hope she was right. May this book enrich and deepen your life, as much as writing it has mine.

INTRODUCTION

Many authors create titles for their work after it is written, but I established my title at the outset. I wanted to write a deeply personal book, not about the things I had come to know at an intellectual level, but about what I had come to know in the depths of my being. In mid-life, I came to understand that the most significant movements in my life had less to do with the places I had gone, and the things I had done, than with the *deepening* that had occurred within. I wanted to capture that in my book, and this is the reason I chose the title *A Deepening Life*.

Although it is cliché to say that life has many lessons to teach, I propose that it is in recognizing the inalienable truth behind this cliché, and opening ourselves up fully to life's lessons, that we become more conscious and experience greater freedom. This, in turn, allows us to live more richly, more compassionately, and more deeply. Life experiences, both joyful and sorrowful, are ultimately invitations to reflect and to engage in soulful dialogue with self and others. Out of this interaction, new insights and understandings are gained, and wisdom is born.

As we move within, doors open that allow us to connect with our essence, our *spirit-being* — our divine self. It is in relationship to self, to one another, and to the world around us, that we have the capacity to experience a deep connection, a "knowingness," an intimacy with God, no matter what name we give to this Presence in our lives.

I have spent the past five years consciously reflecting on my life, and this book is the fruit of that reflection. In these pages I share the wisdom gleaned from the lessons I have learned thus far on my life's journey. Each chapter reveals a particular theme that has held prominence in my life, and has enlarged my soul. This is my story of a *deepening life*.

It is my conviction that in a spirit of humility and grace we are called to teach one another, for wisdom gained is not only intended for the transformation of self, but for the transformation of the world. It is for this reason that I openly share my thoughts with you in this book. May my words enrich your life, and inspire you to reflect on the important lessons you have learned and are called to teach others.

I have chosen to fold a number of journal entries (they are *italicized*) into my book, because they reveal the raw truth of my thoughts and feelings. You will notice that in the final chapter of my book, I begin to use the word God and *Sophia* interchangeably to refer to the Divine. *Sophia* is the Greek word for wisdom. In biblical wisdom texts, divine wisdom is personified in the feminine. Using any name or metaphor for God will always prove inadequate, given the impossibility of describing and capturing the fullness of God, but in order to share a deeply personal relationship with her I find it helpful to use a name. As I moved into mid-life my soul began to resonate with *Sophia,* divine wisdom. *Sophia* is the way I come to God and the way God comes to me. Saying "yes" to her invitation to wisdom, humility, and grace has been a profound blessing in my life.

At the end of each chapter are a series of reflective questions intended to help you grow in consciousness and deepen *your* life. I invite you to keep a journal close at hand so you may record your thoughts as you spend time with each question. Reflecting on your own life will enable you to cull the wisdom *you* have learned on your life's journey, and will, I hope, inspire you to share those insights with others. In sharing the wisdom of our unique life lessons, we challenge and enlighten, and move one another to deeper consciousness. In this place, we live closer to our divine selves and are inspired to live more kindly and more gently, and we create space for others to do the same.

Growing in consciousness and deepening our lives is an extraordinary gift we give to the world, because our individual evolution of consciousness has immeasurable impact on the expanding consciousness of humanity as a whole. May this book inspire you to live more consciously and more deeply, so that you leave a compassionate mark on others and on the world.

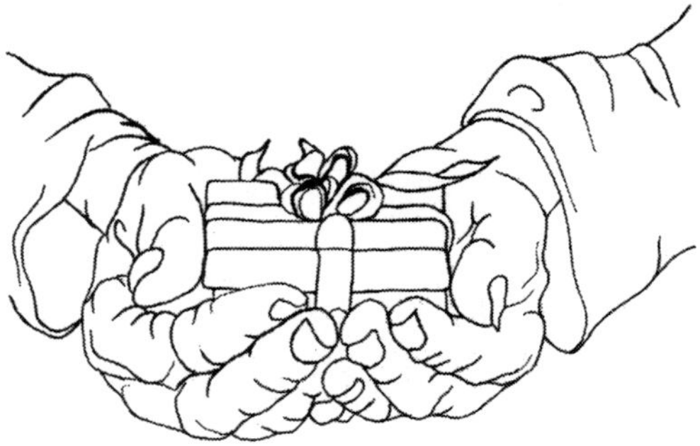

CHAPTER ONE

Unexpected Gifts

JOURNEY WITH MY FATHER

Some of the most valuable and profound lessons we learn in life are born of struggle and pain. Perhaps no more acutely has this proven true for my own life than when I, with my family, accompanied my father through a ten-year battle with Alzheimer's disease. This incredibly painful experience taught me lessons and graced me with insights that continue to inform my life today.

How odd, perhaps, to begin a book about a *deepening life* with a story about death. This is an irony I acknowledge and embrace, for it is often in relationship to death that life comes together most. The death of a loved one reminds us of what is essential. It draws life into immediate perspective and creates an opportunity to learn profound lessons. We always have the choice whether to sit at the foot of death and reap its wisdom, or to run from its midst as if it can be eluded. When facing my father's illness and death I chose to sit and be taught, and now am sharing the insights I gained from that significant event in my life. In the process of helping to "walk my dad home," I encountered many unexpected gifts.

My dad, Fred, was a man well revered and loved by all family members. Full of life and vitality, he was a very good man at his core. He loved people and always had a funny quip to offer, even to strangers. He endeared people to himself quickly. He was a man who spoke his mind, a "what you see is what you get" kind of person. He spoke forthrightly and honestly, even when he knew his words would meet resistance. For this reason, not everyone was his fan — but I sure was, as was his wife, his other four daughters, his sons-in-law, his grandkids, and his great-grandkids. My father was not a saint or model of perfection, but he was authentic. He was alive with life: genuine, fun loving, and supremely kind.

At first the signs of my father's Alzheimer's were quite subtle. He would repeat himself and get confused, but as the years unfolded we watched his health steadily decline. It became an emotional battlefield as my father fought to preserve every ounce of memory he could secure. We who loved him stood helplessly at the sidelines, watching him literally lose his mind piece by piece. Alzheimer's brings pain and grief, not only to people who have the disease, but to those who love them. In a very real sense my entire family had Alzheimer's, because its effects were far-reaching, devastating, and horrific for all of us. It is an incredibly cruel disease. When my father battled Alzheimer's, we who loved him fought our own private battles as we faced the gradual loss of a man we dearly respected and loved. Like a flashlight battery dimming over the years, the light in my dad's eyes began to fade.... then fade some more... then even more. Slowly but surely, we lost increasingly more of him. I knew that eventually my father's memory of those he loved, including me, would be completely lost. That was not a day I looked forward to.

I keep a journal, a free-flowing narrative of my thoughts and reflections about self, relationships, and life in general. At this particular time in my life, my journal was strewn with words describing my struggle to accept that, a little more each day, I was losing my dad to a horrific disease. I remember well the spring evening when, with profound sadness in my heart, all I wrote in my bedraggled journal was one short line:

Today my father did not know me.

Earlier that day I had been to the home of one of my sisters, to attend a wedding shower for a niece. As the shower drew to an end, my father joined us for lunch. He turned and asked me about my wedding. I was his unmarried daughter. Clearly the day had come when my father did not know who I was. I knew this day would be inevitable, but the intellectual preparation I had done in my head did little to protect me from the emotional tsunami that pounded in my heart and flooded my soul when the day actually arrived. It was a tearful drive home. My mind wandered back to five years earlier when my father was first diagnosed... One of my sisters had told me that as a family we had a very long journey ahead of us. As a physiotherapist working with the elderly, she had seen many families navigate this difficult road. My sister's prediction proved completely right.

The person accompanying my father most closely through his illness was my mother. She was strength incarnate as she cared for my dad tirelessly for eight years in our family home. As I said earlier, Alzheimer's disease does not just steal from the people who are afflicted, it exacts a toll on all those who love them. My four sisters and I were very concerned for my father, but as his symptoms increasingly worsened, we worried equally about the wear and tear his disease was inflicting on our mother.

My father began to experience falls and at times wandered, which eventually made it impossible to keep him safe at home.

It was at that point that my mother was forced to make what she would later identify as the most difficult decision of her life. She placed my dad's name on a waiting list for long-term care. I was at the family kitchen table the day the health care representative handed my mom the form that needed her signature to formalize the process. I watched her carefully, acutely aware of how difficult a day this must be for her. As she put pen to paper, in her eyes I saw profound sadness, and an element of disbelief: How could it possibly come to this? I was quite sure that my mother felt as if she was signing over her life.

The health care representative said it could be up to a year before my father would be placed into a long-term care facility, but, almost six months to the day, we got a call that they had a room for him. My sisters and I had previously decided that when the day came we would not let our mother take our father to the long-term care facility alone. We would make this very difficult walk together as a family. The night before we were to place my father into care, I stayed overnight at my parents' home. I did not sleep much. I kept thinking about the fact that this would be the last time my dad would sleep beside his wife in his own bed, in his own home. I worried for my mother and thought about how devastating it would be for her to look over at him in the night knowing this would be their final time sleeping together as husband and wife. I am sure she wanted that night to last as long as possible. I know I did.

It is hard to fully describe what that early morning was like when I heard my mother get up and go to the back bedroom to pack up several suitcases with my dad's clothing. I cannot capture in words the experience of seeing her sit beside him in the bed they had shared for fifty-eight years, and tell him that she could no longer keep him safe at home, and therefore had to take him somewhere else. With her hand rubbing his shoulder she gently explained to him that a long-term care home could now help him more than she could. After all those years of sharing her life with him, she now had to surrender him over. As I stood there and saw my mother's tears, and my dad's confused eyes, I thought my heart would drop through the floor. I could only imagine how gut wrenching that experience must have been for my mother, as she struggled hard to stay strong for him, and I am sure for me as well.

My sisters and I were gathered around the kitchen table in our family home that morning, a morning we had all come to dread. There was a solemnity in the air. Although not wanting to admit it, we knew this would be dad's last moments in a house he had lived in for almost five decades; this was a home he, alongside my mother, had worked hard to turn into a refuge of love and care for his five daughters. As we were cleaning up the kitchen I suddenly felt overwhelmed with emotion, and like a frightened cornered animal I made a quick exit to the back porch.

Moments later my dad came out all dressed and ready to go. He smiled over at me. He had absolutely no idea or understanding of what was transpiring, which made it that much more difficult. He stood right beside me on the porch and we both looked out over the back yard. I pointed to the birds sheltering in the crabapple tree that he had planted many years ago. I told him the story of how tenacious he had been in growing that tree from a tiny root, and how every time he had planted a fresh sprout, the German shepherd next door had found it a delicacy and chewed it to the ground. I explained how he had refused to give up and kept replanting the root, and that this was the reason the tree was standing before us today, sturdy and strong — like my father had been for me all of my life. I looked over at my dad and silently promised him that we would never give up on him either. My family was true to that promise. We made frequent visits to see him in the long-term care home. My mother took driver training and received her driver's licence for the first time at age seventy-five so she could spend time with him every day. Together as a family we cared for him and stood by him to the day he died, fifteen months after we moved him into the facility.

My father crossed over on March 27, 2009. On that sunny Friday morning, my dad's spirit was released. My family was together with him. The belief that what you give to others comes back to embrace you never felt more true. As I looked around the room at the faces of the family members gathered around him, I remember thinking, if I have but one tenth of the love surrounding me on my deathbed, I will be a very lucky woman. My family had embarked on a very long journey together, and now we were surrendering my father over to a better place. Any observer walking by the room that morning would have supposed my tears to be of sadness and loss. Those tears would come, but in that moment my tears were of joy. I was grateful that my father was finally free. I had prayed and wanted that for him for so long. He was a man so full of life and vitality, it killed me to see him unable to function. A number of times when his death was imminent, I whispered in his ear "go and fly free." When he drew his last belaboured breath, I remember looking outside the window and seeing the sun shining. The comforting glow outside reflected the joy and relief I felt on the inside. At his moment of death I could almost hear the shackles that had imprisoned his mind drop to the floor. They no longer had control or power over him. He was finally free. As much as I was incredibly saddened to lose him, I simply could not wish him to continue in the imprisoned state he had been living in for far too long. It was my dad's time to be liberated and return to wholeness. How could those of us who loved him want to take that from him?

It has been over six years since my father's death. I really miss him. Very few days pass when I do not think of him. Tears of loss and sadness wash over me at times, and I do not resist them, for they are the fluid of holy moments and a flowing testimony to the breadth of the love my dad and I shared. I am extremely grateful for my journey with my father. In his illness he gave me invaluable gifts that I will never forget. They were unexpected gifts that flowed from his battle with Alzheimer's, and have continued to enrich, inform, and deepen my life.

LESSONS LEARNED

One of the gifts my dad's Alzheimer's gave me is an increased understanding and appreciation of the magnitude and power of unconditional love. My mother's care of my father throughout his debilitating illness became the profound carrier of this insight. Because of the nature of his illness, much of our family's time and attention had to be given to him. It has only been since my dad's death that I have had the time to truly appreciate the caretaking role my mother assumed in walking beside him every step of the way through his disease.

Time brings perspective, and as I reflect back on the ten years of my father's illness, it is clear that my mom was the unsung hero. It was she who humbly loved and cared, and gave beyond measure. Every day, she faced my father's disease, with all its complexities, both bravely and courageously. My mother taught, and continues to teach, lessons to our family about tenacity, unconditional love, and living faithfully.

I had a front row seat to witness my mother's inner strength, courage, and love. She shouldered the lion's share of my father's disease. Since my dad had fleeting moments where he seemed to know her, she was often on the receiving end of his deepest fears and frustrations. At times he would beg her to help him and ask her why she wasn't doing more to assist him. This was heartbreaking for her, because she was always doing everything in her power to help support him and advocate for his needs. On so many levels it was an incredibly lonely place for my mother, and still is now that he is gone.

My mother's relationship with my father was a powerful witness of what it means to love unconditionally. Her commitment to my father boldly challenges the "disposable love" mentality that frequently manifests itself in present day relationships. My mom's persistence, level of self-sacrifice, and loyalty to her vow of "for better or worse" was humbling to witness. At times I wonder if I will ever love someone as unconditionally as my mother loved my father. It will take a lifetime for me to live out the answer to that question. My mom continues to forge ahead, and she extends to all family members the unconditional love she gave my father. The witness of her quiet, confident, unwavering love is truly inspiring.

There were a number of other unexpected gifts my father's Alzheimer's offered, one of which was a sober reminder to live in the present. Due to his illness my father's recollection of the past was completely gone, and he had no ability whatsoever to imagine a future. The only thing my father had left was the present. In this way, his life became a reminder of the importance of focusing on the present moment. Admittedly in my life I have found this difficult. At times I have been overly focused on the future. When I was in high school I eagerly anticipated striking out on my own at university. When I was in university I could not wait to get my first teaching job and set up my own apartment. Once I had been teaching for a number of years, I was keenly focused on buying my own house. Even now I find myself getting caught up in the whirlwind of a future-driven cycle. As I near retirement from my job as a high school vice-principal, I find myself fantasizing about what life will be like when I no longer have to get up and go to work, and can enjoy life from the seat of my kayak. Talk about wishing one's life away!

My dad's disease served as a wake-up call, a knock on my soul reminding me to revel in the joys to be found each day. It helped me to stop and be present towards my life, and towards all that is going on around and within me. To be present towards that person who stops to talk to me in the grocery store, when all I want to do is grab my items and make a mad dash for home! I may have a kernel of wisdom for them, or they for me. How important it is to remember to stop, listen, and just *be*, so we do not miss the opportunity to be there for another person who, without our knowledge, may desperately need kind eyes and a warm smile to renew their hope in humanity and in life. My father's Alzheimer's reinforced a necessary and simple truth. Ultimately we only have the present moment, so it needs to be embraced, celebrated, and treasured.

My father's Alzheimer's reminded me to not put off to tomorrow what can be done today. There are many people who put their dreams on hold, looking to some elusive day far off in the future when their hopes will be fulfilled. They laboriously save every cent they earn so they can travel when they retire, only to develop an incapacitating illness early into retirement that prevents them from ever travelling. They don't apply for a job that would excite and energize them, out of fear of rejection. Perhaps they pass over an opportunity to pursue a relationship that would lead them to further growth and happiness, out of fear of leaving the security of the known.

My father's illness reminded me to take responsibility for my own happiness and not expect life to make its way to me. Some people are passive observers of their own lives. They work under the belief that life is something that happens *to them* rather than created *by them*. They hand over responsibility for their happiness to others, or to fate, instead of making decisions to move their lives forward in new, exciting, and fulfilling ways. When their lives do not magically come together as they had wished or imagined, they blame others or circumstances for their unhappiness. Joy and happiness elude them, and life becomes a disappointment.

Posted in the office of a therapist I used to see was a sign stating: *No one is coming*. I remember that sign today, many years later, because although it contains four simple words, they pack a punch. The message vehemently opposes a victim stance, because in essence it says: Wake up and take responsibility for yourself! The words are a poignant reminder that no one is riding in on a white horse to rescue you. The inner work that needs to be done needs to be done by you. It is no one else's responsibility to create your happiness. No one can make your life better but *you*!

I had a friend, who sometimes out of frustration would say, "My life is an acid bath!" Every time she would make this statement I would try to think of something to say to bring her comfort and hope. In essence, I would move in to rescue her. I now know I would have been a better friend to myself, and to her, if I had had the courage and wisdom to challenge her to self-responsibility by saying, "If you truly feel your life is an acid bath, then for God's sake, get out of the tub!"

We all have the ability to make choices, and people who choose to wait for life to happen to them will be supremely disappointed and disillusioned. Truly, no one *is* coming. We need to make things happen in life, rather than passively wait for life to happen to us. My father's disease reminded me to make life happen *now* because the future may be shorter than we imagine. On a number of occasions my mother has shared how glad she is that she and my father did not wait to enjoy life. Through the years they celebrated life as they went, by thoroughly enjoying their family and friends. They were "winter Texans," frequently trading snow for the sun. Together they played golf and graciously hosted parties and family get-togethers. They laughed with their friends and sang with abandon at pool parties. They joined in the dance of life, instead of sitting and watching idly from the sidelines. It is a good thing they lived in the present, because they had no idea how short their future together would be. Life changes so quickly, which is why it is important to do what you want to do...now!

As well as teaching me to live in the present, and not obsess about the future, my father's disease offered a caution about living in the past. Out of my own imperfection I have made decisions in life that I am not proud of. I have betrayed and hurt good people, and have been visited by guilt and regret because of it. Since my father's illness, however, I have made greater peace with my past. I have made the apologies I needed to make, and have consciously worked on forgiving myself in order to move forward. There is a picture in my bedroom depicting the view from inside a car. Visible in the rear-view mirror is a sign that reads "dead end." It is juxtaposed with a sign seen through the windshield, which reads, "moving on." I keep that picture up in my room to remind me that obsessing about the past is time wasted. Energy expended looking back leaves little energy to experience the joys of the present. It is important to honour the past and learn from it, but once we learn the lessons it has to teach, we need to let it go. It truly is a dead end. I know first-hand how the past can exact a hold on you, but it is important to trust that the emotional struggle to break free is worth it. We need to quit looking in the rear-view mirror. The past is called the past for a reason... it needs to be left there.

When you have a loved one stricken with Alzheimer's, you find yourself asking why they have to suffer so deeply and for so long. My father battled this debilitating disease for an entire decade. Even the last week of his life seemed to drag on, which made me wonder why relief did not come sooner. I often grappled with why he had to get this horrific disease in the first place. He was such a good man, and it felt so unfair. It still does. I have no answers to these questions, nor do I expect any soon, but what I do know is that my father's suffering had unexpected gifts to bring to those of us who loved him. One of those gifts was helping my family members find our tears.

When getting to know us, one of the questions people frequently ask is whether or not we come from a close-knit family. Without much thought I have always answered "yes," but I feel it was only in pulling together to deal with my father's illness that my family *truly* became close. Part of the reason we pulled together was mere survival. Watching a person you love gradually disintegrate before your eyes is not an easy task, and quite frankly, we needed each other. But, it was more than that. My father's suffering put us in tune with our emotions, and this was a healthy gift for each of us. My experience of our family system (and I acknowledge that other family members may have experienced things differently) is that we are not comfortable expressing certain emotions. As a child, my experience was that sadness and anger were not welcome guests in our home. This is not intended as a criticism, it is simply my experience and observation looking back. Without exception my family members have a well-developed sense of humour, and I do not believe this is a coincidence. We use humour as a coping mechanism to mask deeper feelings we find hard to express, or that we feel are unacceptable. My father's illness broke open the door and freed my family to be sad and to be angry, and more importantly, to be able to express and share these emotions among ourselves. Throughout my father's illness, family members began to talk to one another on a heart level. After our visits with my dad we would share how tough it was to see him become increasingly weak and vulnerable. Whenever we saw faint glimpses of "the old dad" shine through, we would share these stories as a way of giving each other hope that our father was still in there somewhere. And we were also able to freely weep at his bedside, as we knew the final days and hours were imminent. Today we are able to talk about how we still miss him, and express our anger about why such a good man had to die from such a terrible disease. My dad's disease rendered each of us emotionally vulnerable. Out of that vulnerability we found our tears, and in doing so not only became stronger individuals, but grew stronger as a family. I am abundantly grateful to my father for giving us the gift of tears, for I know that in their flowing, grace, healing, and strength are found for the journey ahead. Not long after my father died I paid tribute to my tears in my journal:

I had many tears today. I knew they were bound to come and that eventually they would dawn my doorstep. I opened the door and welcomed them, as I would any visitor. I invited them to sit down and spend time in my midst, teach me their lessons, and be on their way.

My father's disease also offered me the gift of knowing the importance of surrender. I considered myself a control freak, and one of the ways I created the illusion of control was by hyper-organizing my life, my home, and my work. There is, however, nothing like the experience of having a devastating disease invade the body of someone you love to remind you just how little control you actually have. When this happens, you are forced to accept your limitations and surrender control.

Surrendering control brings its own gifts, one of which is a feeling of freedom. Once you acknowledge that there is not a thing you can do about the situation itself, you are free to surrender and use your energy to care for and support your loved one as he or she journeys through the devastating situation. Some people mistakenly view surrendering as *giving up*, but surrendering is really about *giving over.* It is about giving over the belief that we can make all things happen, and that if we try hard enough we can do anything. This is simply not true. *Giving over* is the healthy acknowledgement of one's limitations. It involves making the choice to surrender the illusion of control, and put one's energy in a direction where it can have a positive impact. My family had to surrender to the fact that my father was dying of Alzheimer's, and mobilize our collective energy to support him and each other through a very difficult time.

As you watch someone you love die slowly, you realize that your whole life ultimately leads to the place where you are asked to surrender it all. This is a hard knock to the ego, which rebels and continues to attempt to control. Eventually, the ego is wrestled to the ground and has no other choice but to give up. The impending death of one you love cuts to the core, showing you what is really important and where security truly lies, which is not in the ego-driven things we spend so much time trying to achieve, attain, and protect. It lies in humbly surrendering to the awesomeness and abiding mystery of life, which far surpasses human reason and understanding. In the end, death asks us to hand over everything and trust that in doing so we will live anew.

I am incredibly grateful for the unexpected gifts my father and his disease taught my family. Life lessons, or gifts as I call them, are always there for the reaping, but to reap them you have to show up. When visiting my dad in the long-term care facility I was struck by how many Alzheimer patients had no one coming to see them. Routinely, as part of my visit, I would push my father up and down the halls in his wheelchair. This is when I would see patients all alone in their rooms for extended periods of time. It was very disheartening and sad, so I would wheel my dad into some of their rooms and share a song we had been singing together. It never ceased to amaze me that although my father could not remember any names or places, he could still recall every single word of the familiar old songs. Perhaps it is true that music leaves a permanent mark on the soul.

Never one to sing solo before, my father had become a real songster and put his unique spin on lyrics. Many evenings as we wheeled around the home, I would hear the quiet snickers of support workers as they became privy to his special rendition of songs. Most apt to draw a smile was his big finish for *A Bicycle Built for Two:* "And I'll be damned if my ass you'll jam on a bicycle built for two!" He was a real character. Thankfully, even Alzheimer's could not take that away from him. My mother said that he never forgot the things she would have preferred him to forget!

One evening as my dad and I did our rounds, I ran into a woman near the nurse's station. We exchanged pleasantries and she explained to me that she had just had a visit with her mother. I knew most of the Alzheimer's patients, and had become fairly familiar with their families, but I had never seen this woman before, so I asked if she lived out of town. She told me she lived a few miles away and explained that she did not come to see her mother often because "It is just too hard for me to see her his way." Then she added, "My mother doesn't know me anyway, so it makes no difference." As I watched the woman turn to leave I felt badly, not only for her mom who was left alone most of the time, but for this woman as well. Her mother and Alzheimer's had so many lessons to teach, but she would not be there to learn them. It seemed to me a lost opportunity on so many levels.

As I heard her speak the words "It is just too hard for me to see her this way," I felt myself become judgmental. No one enjoys seeing a loved one suffer, and no one in their right mind freely invites pain into their life. The reality is, however, that loved ones *do* experience suffering, and when they do it seems to me it should not be about us, but about them. Still, I needed to remind myself that it is important, particularly in difficult situations, to remain open and not judge. I had no knowledge of the nature of the relationship this daughter had shared with her mother before Alzheimer's. There could have been tension for years between them, which could explain why she did not visit her mother very often. Clearly it was not my place to allocate blame, so I consciously reminded myself to shift from a place of judgment to a place where I could connect and empathize with this daughter. I was able to do this by reminding myself how painful it feels to be unrecognized by your own parent.

In the final four years of my father's life, he did not know me. When I would visit him in the long-term care home, he frequently thanked me for caring for him, thinking I was simply one of the workers. From my perspective, whether or not my dad knew me was not the point. *The point was that I knew him.* He was still my father, even if he no longer remembered me as his daughter. When I visited him, what he *did* know is that a caring person was enjoying his company and spending time with him. In my mind, that was more than enough reason to visit.

Like the daughter I mentioned above, some children of parents with Alzheimer's do not believe their father or mother ever recognizes them. I am not convinced this is always the case. In fact I believe that some people with Alzheimer's have breakthrough moments when they recognize their loved ones. I experienced this with my father in what would end up being my second-last visit with him before his death. On that particular evening, I lay stretched out toward the foot of his bed. He was in his wheelchair, parked beside me. As I turned to reach for the TV remote, I saw my father's right hand move slowly toward me. The back of his hand found its way to my left cheek, and as he looked at me he rubbed the back of his hand ever so gently up and down my face. He then moved his hand from my cheek to the top of my hand, and patted it lovingly. I looked back at him, and through tears said, "I love you too, dad." It was a profoundly tender moment. There was a level of "knowingness" on his part when he reached out to me. No one will ever convince me otherwise. To this day I cannot express how supremely grateful I am for that one moment. The retelling of that story still brings tears to my eyes, and my guess is it always will. I am glad I showed up for my father, and he for me.

One of the sources of hope and happiness amidst all the pain was being able to watch my father continue to touch people's lives, even from behind the veil of Alzheimer's. His songs, funny quips, and abiding care for others all continued to his dying days. On his deathbed, as he surveyed the large number of family members gathered around him, he turned and asked my mom how much money she was charging per head for "the show." We all laughed. My father was an accountant, so it seems that once an accountant always an accountant, even to the end!

I prayed many prayers throughout the years of my father's illness, and I always requested the same two things. First, that my dad would have some recognition and memory of my mother to his dying day, and second, that he would never lose his sense of humour. Thankfully, both prayers were answered. One afternoon, on what would end up being one of his final days, he woke up temporarily and slowly turned his head to face my mother. He whispered something in her direction, and in an attempt to ascertain what he was saying, my mother lowered her ear to his lips. He gently kissed her, told her he loved her, and asked her to pray for him. This would be one of the last conscious interactions he would share with his soulmate of near sixty years.

On the day of my father's death, the funeral director made a point of telling my mom that although he had removed many deceased persons from that facility, he had never seen so many staff go out of their way to come and say a final goodbye as they had for my father. Clearly, we were not the only people who had been taught important life lessons by my father: he had left unexpected gifts for others too.

I am immeasurably grateful for having been part of my father's living, and of his dying. Both have been grace. From the depths of his illness and suffering, he provided me with significant opportunities for growth and deepening. It was a humbling experience and a profound privilege to learn lessons from my father right to the end.

A father with young children scampering along the shoreline... whirlwind of sand. Little feet lead, older feet follow. Giggles, laughter, pride, the stuff of deep love. Takes me back to Port Dover...my father slowly wading into the water, cradling me in front like a bundle of wood, my wee arms clinging to him. A brief but dramatic countdown...3...2...1...the excitement builds! I am lifted high, catapulted forward, and fed merciless to the waves. My father's laughter, the first audible sound as my head punctures the watery surface. I swim hastily back in his direction... "Throw me again dad, throw me again!"

Oh, why do suns have to set on days like these? Why do suns have to set on fathers' lives?

Deepening Your Life…

What have been the death experiences in your life? Loss of a job, loss of a significant relationship, loss of your health, the death of a loved one…

What were the unexpected gifts these death experiences offered?

In what ways have you deepened from these experiences?

What do you find most difficult to surrender? Your need for control, feelings of anger or regret, hurtful memories, the pain of loss…

Where do you live most of your life — in the past, the present, or the future?

What has been a tender moment in your life? What was it about this moment that moved you?

Who have been the unsung heroes in your life, and how have they made a difference?

Who or what in your life do you still need to "show up" for?

How might the people, places, and events of your life be calling you to grow and change, so that you enjoy greater personal freedom and a deepened life?

CHAPTER TWO

The Path of Integrity

A REDISCOVERY OF SELF

I share many soulful dialogues with friends, and am known to pose provocative questions that will spark discussion. One summer, at a campfire with friends, I suggested we go around the circle and everyone share what they thought each of us would deem as important to be said at our funeral. I am not sure why on a clear crisp summer night I was led to ask this particular question, but I was. My friends have learned over the years that it is easier to humour me and go along with my "game of life" questions, as I call them, than to bother to resist!

Each of us entered the experience of that night's particular "game of life" question with thoughtfulness and sincerity of heart. As we made our way around the friendship circle, I sat poised and curious when it came time for my friends to share what they thought I deemed most important to be said upon my death. "Integrity," one of my friends said. "I think you want people to remember you as a person of integrity." Nodding their heads, my other friends concurred. My head nodded as well, because I felt my friend had hit the nail on the head. Integrity *is* supremely important to me. I feel that without it, people do not live out their truth or fully actualize the person they are capable of becoming. That said, striving to live with integrity has been the biggest challenge I have faced in my life. For me, it has always come with a cost.

Up until about thirty years of age I never gave conscious thought to integrity per se. I had always strived to be a good person, having been raised in a faith-filled household that instilled clear morals and values. I attended a Catholic elementary school and a Catholic high school. I studied at several Catholic universities; after training as an educator, I assumed the position of teacher at a Catholic high school. In my twenties I preoccupied myself with the same things other people my age did. I bought my first car, set up my first apartment, and enjoyed travelling to a few places I told myself I would explore once I had a full-time job. It was not until my early thirties that I found myself facing questions that forced me to look integrity straight in the eye. I was becoming increasingly aware that one important piece of my life was not falling into place — a committed relationship with a man.

I had met and dated a number of wonderful men, a few of whom were interested in pursuing a long-term relationship, one of them marriage, but something did not feel right. Although I felt very comfortable around men and thoroughly enjoyed the company of opposite-sex colleagues and friends, developing a romantic relationship with a man was a struggle for me. No matter how hard I tried (and trust me, I tried) I never had the same feelings for the men I dated as they had for me. This made me feel awkward, inadequate, and abnormal. Time and time again I would ask myself why I could not make a relationship with a man work, especially when there was nothing I wanted more than to marry and have a family. Over time I began to beat myself up for not being able to do what my sisters, cousins, and friends were doing, as one by one they got married. I was a bridesmaid in a number of their weddings, and although I was happy for them, the whole experience served to heighten how abnormal I felt for not being able to make a relationship with a man work. I remember the alienation, loneliness, and pain of those years.

Eventually I grew tired of feeling inadequate and made the decision to begin counselling so I could try to discern what was at the root of my struggles. Stepping into such unexplored territory felt very scary, but thankfully my counsellor, Gloria, was open, welcoming, and supportive. She provided a safe haven for me to begin to open up and risk asking important questions about my sexuality. It was after a number of months of counselling, many soulful talks with good friends, much conscious discernment, and the gradual erosion of psychological defences, that at age thirty-three I acknowledged for the first time that I was gay. The issue of integrity now took a front seat as I faced the choice of either embracing who I was as a gay woman, or turning my back on who I was and living my life according to the perceived comfort level of others.

It was disconcerting to find myself at this particular crossroads at age thirty-three. I did not share the experience many gay persons have had, of knowing from an early age they are gay. I certainly recall feeling different from other girls. I never enjoyed participating in stereotypical female activities, like skipping rope or dressing dolls. I identified more with the boys in my neighbourhood, and had more interest in their activities like building forts, riding bikes, and playing sports. Unlike most of my girlfriends, I did not get excited about shopping for what I would refer to as "girlie girl" clothes (I still call them that today!), and much preferred clothing that was sport-friendly. I still remember a pair of running shoes my parents bought me that had the National Hockey League logo emblazoned on the top. I absolutely loved those shoes, and it is only now, over forty years later, that I truly appreciate the freedom my parents provided me in letting me wear the clothes that felt most "me," instead of insisting I wear clothes deemed *appropriate* for girls.

Looking back, I can see the signs, connect the dots, and without doubt recognize that I was gay from a very early age; it just took a significant period of time for me to name that reality for myself. This raises the question: Why did I not make the connection? I truly believe that I, and many other gay persons in my age group, would have identified earlier if being same-sex oriented had been presented as an acceptable and healthy way to identify. In doing so I would have been spared much internal angst and self-loathing, trying to feel "normal" by attempting to make heterosexual relationships "fit." The topic of homosexuality, as it was most commonly referred to when I was young, was not something people talked about. For example, I do not remember homosexuality ever being talked about at school. This is interesting, given that I attended Catholic schools whose lessons often addressed moral issues, of which homosexuality was one. In light of what the Catholic Church teaches about homosexuality, perhaps it was best that my school skipped those lessons!

I heard very little about homosexuality at home. Both of my parents were raised Catholic, and the Church at that time took a *love the sinner hate the sin* approach. It seems to me that my parents were ahead of their time. I do not recall them ever saying anything negative about people who were gay. I never heard them attach any of the morally laden terms, such as sin or abomination, to the word homosexual. When the topic did get raised at home, I remember homosexuality being presented as a sickness, as something a person could not help, and therefore, homosexual people were not to be judged or made to feel responsible for being ill. I think this may be one of the reasons I never made the connection that I was gay. Although I felt different from other girls, I did not feel sick in any way.

Growing up I was aware of an older cousin who was rumoured to be gay. My sisters and I would giggle somewhat uncomfortably about it on our way over to visit her family every Christmas Eve. My cousin is an exceptionally gentle person with a very kind heart, so I felt guilty snickering behind her back. She was always very good to me. I specifically recall one Christmas visit when she spent time showing me how to play a guitar chord. In a room full of adults, busily engaging one another in conversation, my cousin took the time to pay attention to me. I did not see this cousin often, but when our families spent time together I always really enjoyed her company. Even though I felt quite connected to her, I never said much about it to my family. Perhaps on a very unconscious level I was worried about guilt through association. Many years later, it was this same cousin (whom I would come to know as not gay but transgender) who became a tremendous ally in helping me name and come to terms with who I was as a gay woman. Today we are friends as well as cousins.

Throughout adolescence and into young adulthood, I remained unaware of being gay. Looking back there were clear signs of the emotional dissonance I was experiencing. The fact that I had to drink alcohol and get a "buzz on" in order to kiss boyfriends good night should have been a clue! I honestly felt I had just not yet met the right man yet. I believed that one day I would meet the man intended for me, marry him, and start a family; in this way all the pieces of my life would finally fall into place.

In my second year of university, seemingly out of the blue, I fell into a deep depression that lasted nine months. I am struck now at the irony of the length of time. What was gestating within me for nine months? What new life was trying to be born in me that I was not ready to look at, let alone embrace? At the time I had absolutely no idea why I was feeling so profoundly sad and detached from self. It did not make logical sense. I had adapted well to my studies at university, had made new friends while away at school, and everything was fine at home. So why was I feeling so depressed and despondent? I honestly did not know what was going on inside of me, and have rarely talked openly to family and friends about this period of my life. I know that depression, or any mental illness, is still a relatively taboo topic, but this is not the reason I have avoided sharing my experience. I am not ashamed or embarrassed to have experienced depression. It was an extremely sad, lonely, and scary time in my life, and it led me to a very dark place. Perhaps the reason I don't talk about it much is that there is still pain in the retelling.

It is interesting, what memories we carry over time and what stays in our heart. I remember Christmas morning of the year of my depression. I recall waking up in the back bedroom of my family's home and hearing the muffled voices of family members gathered in the kitchen. I heard their laughter wafting down the hallway as I lay in bed crying. The dichotomy was overwhelming. My family was so happy, but I felt so sad. I remember thinking that I did not want to live anymore. I had felt so sad and tired for so long that I just wanted it to stop, but I did not know how to get better because I was unaware of what had made me so depressed.

That Christmas morning I got up out of bed and wiped away my tears. When I felt confident that my eyes would not betray me, I made my way to the living room where our usual Christmas morning ritual of unwrapping gifts would begin. That year my parents surprised me with a white ten-speed bike. It was a very thoughtful gift. A brand new bike is a rarity when you have four older sisters! I remember consciously putting on my *"Tis the season to be jolly"* face so no one would know that I was hurting. I was grateful to be able to rely on my fine acting abilities. They were well polished: I had used them at school for the past half year to hide my depression. I couldn't tell my family about my feelings, because they would ask me to explain the reason, and I had no clue. Wouldn't they, too, wonder what I had to be depressed about? After all, I had a loving family, good friends, and was doing well at university — although there had been a definite decrease in my grade average during this time period.

Over time, I have come to understand that the lingering depression I experienced at age twenty-one was intricately connected to the unconscious repression of my sexual orientation. Since I was not psychologically prepared to let down my defences and face the fact that I was gay, I was spending an inordinate amount of energy repressing who I truly was. This left no room for joy in my heart. I own a picture taken during that period of my life, and in it I am standing next to a friend and feigning a smile. I look gaunt, pale, and profoundly sad. If you look close enough you can actually see the stress lines in my forehead and face. Still today, I do not like looking at that picture. I keep it out of sight in a box, stored in my closet. The irony of its placement is not lost on me! A number of times throughout the years I have come upon that picture and thought about throwing it away. After all, who wants to be reminded of such a sad time in life? Who wants a pictorial representation of one's dark night of the soul? Yet I have chosen to keep it, because it is part of who I am and where I have been. That profoundly difficult time in my life has helped form the person I am today. Having walked that painful terrain made me a more compassionate person — a wounded healer.

And what of my Christmas bike? About five years later, I began tour cycling and needed to purchase a bike that was lighter to peddle and would allow me to carry gear. Around the time of my new bike purchase, a colleague borrowed my Christmas bike, liked it, and asked if she could buy it from me. That bike had been a generous gift to me, and I in turn made it a gift to her. I love my parents dearly for their love and thoughtfulness in buying that bike for me, but it would be dishonest to say I missed it when it was gone from my basement. Now when I made trips downstairs I no longer saw the white frame that reminded me of that very sad time in my life. No longer was I reminded of the guilt I had felt for not being in the emotional space to fully appreciate the generous gift my parents gave me that Christmas morning in 1982.

It wasn't until early in the third decade of my life that I was able to gather enough ego security to let down my defences and come out. Straight friends often ask what it is like to come out to family and friends, but they do not realize that what is most difficult is the first step, coming out to self. For me, it felt incredibly unsettling to be thirty-three and only then acknowledging, naming, and struggling to accept a core truth about myself. It felt like a resurgence of adolescence as I grappled with my sexual identity, and tried to "re-understand" myself, to embrace who I was all over again. It was unnerving and disorienting, and the whole process left me feeling extremely vulnerable.

Amidst the emotional unsettledness, I was forced to ask important questions related to personal integrity. Do I live out of who I now know myself to be, or do I try and repress, now at a conscious level, who I am in order to please my family, the Church, and the world around me? I had struggled long and hard to accept myself as a gay woman, and I did not want to turn my back on self. Now that I had finally accepted who I was, I wanted to be authentic and walk the path of integrity by being totally open and honest with others, but the fear of rejection by those I loved and respected felt overwhelming.

I noticed that as I came to accept myself for who I was, I experienced greater inner freedom and felt more connected spiritually. Coming out within helped connect me more deeply with God. I believed that God fashioned me as a gay person, and delighted in me. I had no doubt in my mind or my heart that God loved and accepted me as I was. I had no issues with God, nor did I feel God had issues with me. Being honest with myself gave me a clearer glimpse of my own divinity, and allowed me to more fully experience the Divine presence that had creatively and generously planted that divinity within me. I felt good about myself and was finally at peace with who I was. Where I felt anxiety and fear was in thinking about how to tell the people I loved most that I wasn't who they thought I was. Of course I knew deep down I was still the same person, but I was not sure the people who loved me would see it that way. It was my deep-rooted relationship with God, and the support of close gay friends, that gave me the strength to move forward.

Some gay people do not feel it is important to tell their parents about their sexual orientation, and I believe this choice always needs to be respected. For me, it was an issue of honesty and integrity. I did not want to live a lie. My family is integral to my life, and has been highly influential in forming who I have become as a person. I needed my family to know who I *truly* was. I had deep trust in my loved ones, and was fairly confident I would not be rejected, but I was still afraid. I had heard enough devastating "coming out to parents" stories to shake my confidence and cast doubt on how it would all play out. Some gay friends had shared with me their hurtful experiences of being rejected by the very family members they believed would be the most open-minded. This incited fear, and delayed my coming out to family members for some time.

It was almost a year into my first relationship with a woman before I finally felt ready to take the risk of telling my parents I was gay. "Ready" is not the most honest word, because I don't think I ever truly felt ready, but I knew in my heart I was as ready as I would ever be. Since my partner and I were quite connected socially, I had increasing fears that family members would hear I was gay from an outside source. I wanted my family members to hear it from me first.

The primary reason it was important for me to tell my family that I was gay was that I was tired of hiding a big part of my life from the people I loved most. My integrity was taking a beating from the fact that I was living a lie. I was increasingly dissatisfied with having to skirt around my gay relationship in conversations with family members. My Sunday evening routine involved calling home and speaking with my mother. Equally routine was her asking me what I had been up to that past week. My heart would feel heavy. I wanted to tell my mom the truth that my partner and I had enjoyed a nice week together, but instead I would fabricate events shared with straight friends to cover up my gay relationship. Each time I did this, I felt horrible. I absolutely hated lying to my mother. I owed her more. I owed myself more; it was time to come clean. I had heard a gay man in a television interview say that he did not know what reaction his family and friends would have to his coming out, but he would rather be hated for who he was than loved for who he was not. His words were about personal integrity, and they deeply resonated with me. This interview helped propel me to come out to my parents.

I remember well that it was a Holy Thursday night when I drove home to have dinner with my parents and tell them the truth of who I was. I smile now at my choice of days. Perhaps I was worried that this might be my "last supper" with them? I have no doubt that something unconscious was at work in my choice of that evening. In the Christian tradition, Holy Thursday marks the entrance into the paschal mystery: the life, death, and resurrection of Jesus. Could the timing have been more appropriate? For me, there needed to be a letting go, a death of my old self in order to fully embrace and experience the freedom of an emerging authentic self. For my parents, it meant initiation into the struggle of letting go and letting die the dreams and wishes they had for their "straight Joan," to make room to accept and celebrate their "gay Joan."

As I made the hour-long drive to my parents' home, it struck me that life as they knew it was about to change. It was a gut-wrenching feeling knowing that I was about to hurt, possibly devastate, the two people in life I most wanted to please and protect. I feared risking the withdrawal of love from the people whose love counted the most. It was agonizingly difficult, and I was exceedingly anxious and afraid. I also felt an element of shame, which emanated from all the negative things I had heard said about people who were gay. Obviously I had more work to do to fully accept myself. As I walked through the back door of my family home, I was again struck by the paradox that choosing to be authentic to myself could potentially cost me the love and respect of the people I loved most.

Being rejected in life is a difficult experience no matter what your sexual orientation, but as a gay person, living in a heterosexual world that often misunderstands and even rejects you, it is particularly important that your parents and family do not turn their backs on you. I kept telling myself that my parents loved me and that nothing, not even this news, would get in the way of that love. But then a gnawing feeling of doubt and anxiety would creep in, making me fear the cost of being true to myself.

Yet I am fortunate and blessed, because that evening, when I came out to my parents, I was not received with judgment or hatred, but with love. My mother's first words to me were, "This does not change the way your father and I feel about you." And my father looked at me with soft eyes and very pragmatically said, "It is what it is." Neither of my parents treated me any differently once they knew I was gay. Since my father is now deceased, I am glad I had the opportunity to share with him who I truly was before he died; it is important to me to be loved for who I truly am. I know that at the time I came out to my parents, they did not fully understand same-sex orientation, and my mother has shared a few times since that she accepts me but does not understand my same-sex attraction. I really respect my mother's integrity in being honest, and I do not judge how she feels. After all, it took me thirty-three years to come to understand who I am, so if she needs thirty-three years, that only seems fair! Standing where I do now, what I have come to know in my heart is that what is most important is not what my mother did not understand, but what she did clearly understand, which is that no matter what, you love your children unconditionally.

I do not want to imagine what my life would have been like had I not received love and acceptance from my parents. Rejection by my family would have *totally* devastated me, and quite honestly, I don't think I would have bounced back. I believe I would have plummeted back into a period of depression and might have found a way to remove myself permanently from the pain of loneliness and rejection. My heart feels deeply for gay people who come out and experience rejection from their families. I admire their strength and courage in moving forward without their families' acceptance and support. I recognize that coming out to parents has cost many gay persons a lot more than it cost me. I look to and pray for the day when all gay daughters and sons will be welcomed by their parents with love. As an educator I am committed to doing my part, however small, to make this a reality sooner than later.

LIVING THE TENSION

At the time I came out to myself, I was employed as a department head of religion and family life at a Catholic high school, so now I faced questions of integrity not only on a personal level but on a professional level as well. In its official teaching, the Catholic Church differentiates between homosexual orientation and homosexual activity. In essence, the Catholic Church's official position is that it is okay to be gay, but it is not acceptable to express same-sex attraction on any physical level. In the Catechism of the Catholic Church, homosexual acts are deemed "intrinsically disordered." Clearly my same-sex partnership was unacceptable in the eyes of the Church. So, I wondered — what to do now? Do I continue working within the Catholic school system and the confines of Catholicism's teaching about homosexuality, which demands I be secretive about my relationship? And, if I choose to do this, am I willing to swallow my integrity? Or, do I make an effort to teach in the public school board, where I can live more openly as a gay woman but will no longer be in a position to try to make an impact on the Catholic school system from the inside out, by educating people about this issue and helping to ensure supports are in place for LGBTQ (lesbian, gay, bisexual, transgender, queer) students? I chose to be an educator to try to make a difference in the world, so will leaving the Catholic school board be a cop out? As a person for whom integrity is so important, where is integrity to be found if I choose to walk away from the LGBTQ youth in our board whom I can speak up for and help? If their allies keep leaving the Catholic school system, who will help them fight their battles? These were the types of questions I asked myself during the process of discerning what to do.

I was also concerned about job security. If I stayed working in the Catholic system, my job could be in jeopardy. If the wrong person discovered I was living in a gay relationship and chose to report it, my job could be at risk. This fear made me hyper-vigilant: I spent much time looking over my shoulder, worrying about who might be lurking around the next corner. My partner at the time also taught in a Catholic high school, so even at home we exercised extreme caution. We made sure we were in the house before expressing affection — we were careful not to kiss in front of any window, for fear that someone would see us. When out in public we got anxious if we ran into colleagues or students from one of our school communities. In seeing us side by side, would they put two and two together? Would our secret be out? If so, what would it cost?

The repercussions my gay relationship could have on my job weighed heavily on the minds and hearts of the people who loved me. It was my parents' biggest fear when I first came out to them, and it continues to be a fear held by my mother today. Sadly, this fear is not unfounded. Years ago a teacher friend of mine was fired by an Ontario Catholic school board for marrying his same-sex partner. The forbidden nature of gay relationships in official Catholic teaching puts teachers living in gay partnerships in a precarious position. It renders them incredibly vulnerable, and that was how I was feeling.

It was a very unsettling time. Living my life as a gay woman was conflicting with the religious teachings I had been raised in and had taught for many years. The experience of coming out to myself had been a long struggle, and for the first time in my life things felt like they finally "fit," yet the Catholic Church taught that my most sacred relationship was intrinsically disordered. The burning question for me became, How do I live authentically within this paradox? What does one do when one's lived experience is in direct opposition to the teachings of a religion one has lived by one's whole life? As a religion teacher working in a Catholic school system, I was called upon not only to teach, but also to model the teachings of the Catholic Church. How could I do this knowing in the very fabric of my being that the love I felt for my partner was not wrong, or "disordered" in any way? I wrestled within and seriously questioned how I could continue to work in a school system that taught what it did about gay relationships, and in essence, what it taught about me.

It was a heart-wrenching time as I weighed out what I could live with and what I could not. Ultimately I made the decision to stay and work in the Catholic system. I wanted to try to generate change and make it easier for sexual-minority youth to come out to themselves and others, and to help ensure they would be received with acceptance and love. I decided that although I no longer espoused or personally supported a number of official Catholic teachings (particularly as they pertained to same-sex relationships, the role of women, the hierarchy of the Church, and birth control), there were foundational things I liked about working in a religious context. As a deeply spiritual person, I liked being part of a school system where I did not have to apologize for teaching out of a spiritual worldview. I liked the witness and support of colleagues who were ensuring there was room for God in their lives. I liked working in an educational system that believed in the sacramentality and beauty of all creation, and that held social justice and social action as integral to what it means to be human. I liked that I had the freedom to talk to students about grace, compassion, and God's love, and in doing so pass on to them the hope that comes from believing and knowing that an Abiding Presence has their back, no matter what.

Since coming out to myself, I have continued to work in a Catholic school system for twenty years. The school system I work for strives to be accepting and supportive, but like all Catholic boards it must uphold official Catholic teaching. There have been times, therefore, where I have discovered, often in deeply painful ways, that it is extremely difficult to maintain personal integrity while working within a system that is oppressive towards who you are. One situation in particular stands out in my mind, and will illustrate my experience:

Over ten years ago, a rather lengthy document about homosexuality was distributed within my school board. The author of the document was a Roman Catholic priest. The contextual approach of his section on the Bible and homosexuality was well done. Where the document broke down for me was where it spoke of the psychological and social realities for persons who are gay. At one point, the priest author offered his thoughts on what gay youth should and should not do. Gay youth were advised to refrain from coming out to an ill parent. Homosexual "acts" at one point were referred to as "human weakness." Heterosexist wording was embedded throughout the document, with the frequent use of the phrase "we heterosexuals." Reference was made to a small number of gay people who "promote gay propaganda," and try "to recruit." In the document, gay persons were advised to see their homosexuality as simply one part of who they were, inferring that they could compartmentalize their sexual orientation, as separate from their personhood. I was terribly disheartened by the document, and found it incredibly upsetting. A burning question kept coming to mind as I read it. How does a heterosexual celibate male feel he is in any position to address the gay experience? As a gay woman, I would never begin to assume I could write a document about priestly celibacy, since this is not my lived experience. I think back to my mother and the honesty she showed in admitting she did not understand homosexuality. My mother did the most honest thing, which was to name what she understood and what she did not understand. As a heterosexual, she instinctively knew that she would never fully understand the gay experience, and I deeply respect that she has never pretended to. The heterosexual author of that document would have benefited greatly from wisdom like my mother's in this area.

It is important to humbly name what we know and what we don't know. It is when we presume to understand another person's lived experience, and try to speak *for* them, that we contribute to their oppression. Although this priest intended no harm, it was nevertheless presumptuous and arrogant for him to assume he understood and was in a position to advise persons who were same-sex oriented, as he did not share their lived experience. Nowhere in the document was there evidence that gay persons had been invited to tell *their own* stories. I was so angry and upset about the document that I wrote a lengthy response to the author, which resulted in respectful dialogue back and forth. I know the author to be a kind man, who holds no malice in his heart. His intentions were good. He was trying to address some of the issues that had recently surfaced within the board regarding support for students of a sexual minority. While most clergy at the time were avoiding this hot-button issue, he was at least making an attempt to provide a pastoral response.

What was frustrating for me, however, was not being able to come out to this priest, in order to frame my response to his document as the insights of a gay person. As a teacher, and at this point a religion consultant in a Catholic school board, I did not have the freedom to come out, so I had to frame my critical response using an "objective" voice. Had I had been free to speak openly and honestly, I would have said, "When talking about gay people, you are talking about *me*, and with all due respect you have no lived experience of what it is like to be a gay person and live as an invisible minority in the world, and in the Church, so please stop writing about us and advising us."

As I said earlier, I believe we must exercise extreme caution in assuming we can speak to the lived experience of other people, gay or otherwise. We need to invite people to speak *for themselves*. I firmly believe that the Catholic Church and Catholic school boards need to create spaces where gay persons can safely come forward and candidly share who they are, trusting that they will be listened to and heard. Open and honest dialogue must be a "non-negotiable" if we are to honour and respect people's lived experiences. Dialogue between people of differing sexual orientations would build empathy and understanding. What a difference it would make if we stood on humble ground and invited gay persons to tell their stories, sharing what it is like for them to live in the world. How different this would be from presuming to know how gay people feel, and deciding what is best *for* them. Honest dialogue would move the Church, and Catholic school systems, closer toward the establishment of just and inclusive communities that celebrate the rich diversity and equality of *all* persons, created in goodness by God.

Sadly, the Catholic Church, like many other churches, has yet to fully create the inclusive community modelled by Jesus in the gospels. The institutional Church has yet to invite gay persons to talk openly and honestly about their lives without also insisting that they apologize for who they love. Catholic teaching continues to label gay people's sacred partnerships and physical expressions of love toward one another as *intrinsically disordered*. I believe that the Church would make a more compassionate and significant contribution to the world if it concerned itself more with why people hate than with who they love!

It concerns, disappoints, and saddens me that the institutional Church continues to use its power to shame gay people into silence, because shame is soul defying. It oppresses gay people and makes them feel ungodly. I do not believe God wants any part of shame, because it takes people away from themselves and makes them feel like they are a mistake. To me this is the antithesis of Jesus' desire that people "have life, and have it abundantly." *(John 10:10)*

Failing to reach out to gay people is a profound loss to the Church. Gay persons would bring a unique richness to Church communities if they were invited and welcomed. Many gay people are natural healers who carry deep compassion in their hearts, because as outsiders they have walked a painful path on the margins, and know woundedness all too well. But, gay people's voices continue to be unacknowledged, uninvited, and unwelcomed by the Catholic Church.

The institutional Church needs to abandon its either-or thinking about gay persons. Such thinking demands that they either live celibate lives or be seen as living a morally disordered life. This narrow, limiting, dualistic mentality serves to exclude and devalue people. The Church needs to open its mind and heart to gay persons and adopt thinking that is invitational and inclusive, expanding the soul rather than limiting it. Inviting the voices of gay people to come forward would undoubtedly be unsettling for a Church that has silenced such voices for so long, but in the interests of honouring and respecting all human beings, this needs to happen. It is healthy for Church communities to stay with the difficult questions and work them through, rather than avoid these questions or even disallow them.

Some people hold out hope that the official Catholic Church will one day fully celebrate gay people and their partnerships. I pray they are right, but in order for the Catholic Church to move in this direction I believe it will need to address its deep-seated fear and suspicion of the feminine, a suspicion that makes the Church incredibly fearful not only of women, but of gay men, who for the most part more readily embrace and express both their masculine and feminine energies. Openly gay men are threatening to a Church that has for centuries, both consciously and unconsciously, acted as a haven for some of its priests to hide and avoid dealing with who they are as gay men. True liberation will only come when the Church owns its projections (which are fear based) and faces its systemic shadow (the parts of itself it has denied and does not want to look at). This will take tremendous courage and faith, and demand a significant re-visioning. Real change will only occur through major restructuring of the Church - only in the breakdown will we see a breakthrough.

Pope Francis may well be the leader who brings this new vision. In him I find tremendous hope. He exudes authenticity and seems to possess much integrity. His openness to the people he leads and serves is totally inspiring. Like Jesus, Pope Francis finds himself drawn to the people on the margins. My prayer is that the spirit of inclusion and social justice he embodies, and which appears to animate his papacy, will bring forward the issue of same-sex relationships (as well as other issues of equal importance), so that justice can be attained for *all* God's people. I hope that Pope Francis continues to lead the Catholic Church in a positive direction, so that future gay Catholics will not have to suffer the pain and alienation experienced by so many of us who have gone before them.

VULNERABILITY AND COURAGE

Over the past twenty years I have found it difficult to live authentically as a gay woman within the oppressive confines of the systemic homophobia of which the Church — and therefore the Catholic school system — is embedded. Sometimes the level of frustration, anger, and hurt has been so intense that I have questioned my initial decision to stay and work from within. I experience extended periods of fatigue from the energy drained by suppressing who I am. At times I worry about the toll that working from within is having on me emotionally and physically. I look at the number of gay teachers who have left the Catholic board to teach in the public school system, and I see them living more freely. Many have married and had children (endearingly called *gaybies*). What a tremendous loss it is to Catholic school boards to have incredibly competent and passionate teachers feeling they have no choice but to leave and go work in the public school system. I know a number of people who have made this move, and they are gifted educators who possess deep faith. They loved teaching in a spiritual context within a Catholic school and did not want to leave, but felt they had no other option if they wanted to embrace who they were and live with integrity. The freedom to live life as one chooses is very attractive to me, especially in times when it feels like the oppressive structure I am working within is clipping my wings and suffocating my soul.

Several years back, at the height of frustration and anger, I chose to apply for an elementary administrative position in the public board. I was not granted an interview due the fact that my professional experience was solely at the secondary level. At the time I interpreted this closing door as a sign from God that I was meant to stay put, and continue the work of trying to make a difference in the Catholic school system. Looking back, I honestly do not know if it was truly a sign from God or not, but I do know that there are very few audible voices speaking up for sexual-minority kids in Catholic schools. I also know that God must have gifted me with a strong voice and a stubborn heart for a reason!

It is said that everything has a season and a purpose, and that we will find ourselves in a given time and in a given place for a given reason. I believe this to be true, and feel I was meant to stay and work within the Catholic system to try to help bring about change. Far beyond simply being a job, teaching is my vocation, and planted within this vocation is a desire to give back to others. It is my hope that at the end of my career my contribution as an educator will have had worth far beyond what it ever paid me financially, psychologically, socially, or emotionally. I want my life's work to have served a positive purpose in the lives of others. My work with LGBTQ youth (who at times I refer to as sexual-minority youth) has become an integral part of my teaching vocation. I have a special connection with sexual-minority students because of who I am as a gay woman. There is a *knowingness* and safety that these students find in me. Having experienced the struggle to come out myself, I feel a deep affiliation with these students and deeply respect them. I am struck by their courage and integrity as they try to secure some level of self-esteem amidst the homophobia and transphobia that surrounds them daily. In some ways I am thankful I did not discern I was gay until later in life, because it was hard enough as an adult to come to terms with who I was. By age thirty-three I had many psychological and social supports to draw upon in the coming-out process. Every day I witness how difficult it is for LGBTQ students to navigate their way through all the issues connected with their sexual orientation and/or gender identity, while also dealing with the regular tasks of adolescence. No wonder they have disproportionately higher incidences of depression, suicidal ideation (thoughts about suicide), and completed suicides, than do heterosexual youth.

It is an understatement to say that sexual-minority youth feel vulnerable. As a group, they are frequently rendered voiceless. Over the years, I have worked closely with these students and tried to help them find their voice so they could feel good about themselves from the inside out. For the most part they do not feel understood or welcome at school. Part of my work as an educator has been to strive to bring the issue of support for LGBTQ youth to the forefront, to make the invisible visible.

It should not be surprising that sexual-minority youth feel invisible, given that their lives are rarely reflected anywhere at school. For example, the dating and married relationships they hear discussed in their classes are virtually always heterosexual. The movies they are shown, as complementary lessons in courses, most often depict the lives and issues related to heterosexual persons. The books they read are, for the most part, written by heterosexual authors, and contain predominantly heterosexual characters. The role models suggested to them by teachers are almost exclusively heterosexual historical figures.

Sexual-minority youth encounter this same exclusive world outside the classroom. Smiling out at them from glossy posters pinned up in the hallways are teen heterosexual couples, summoning them to the upcoming school dance. The music they hear played over the PA as they walk to classes, attend assemblies and dances, and travel to and from school on the bus, reflect romantic relationships between men and women. All of these subtle and not-so-subtle messages contribute to LGBTQ youths' feelings of invisibility. Is it any wonder they find themselves asking, "Where am I to be found in my school?"

Heterosexism (the presumption that everyone is or should be heterosexual) contributes to these feelings of invisibility. As a rule, teachers operate under the assumption that all students in their classes are heterosexual. This is not the reality, so sexual-minority students frequently feel excluded, even when this is far from the teacher's intent. I can recall, for example, a visit to my office by a gay male student. He came to see me because he was feeling angry and embarrassed by something that had just happened in his religion class. During a lesson about marriage, his teacher (whom I know to be a competent and caring young teacher) asked all the boys in the class to write down personality characteristics they desired in a woman they might marry one day. Similarly, all the girls were invited to write down the characteristics they would desire in a man. This activity made him feel awkward and left out. He shared with me that he felt forced to pretend to be someone he was not. As a result, even though the class was now over he was still angry.

I had been working closely with this student for a few years and was aware of his anger issues, which began after he came out at home and was rejected. He and I had been exploring ways he might manage his anger in a healthy manner. I knew he enjoyed writing, so one of the strategies I had suggested to him was expressing his anger on paper, as an alternative to pounding his fist into lockers or speaking disrespectfully to teachers. He explained to me that he had used the writing strategy in class that morning, and while the other students spent time listing the personality characteristics they desired in the opposite sex, he scribbled down a few words about how he was feeling. When I asked if I might read what he had written, he timidly pulled a tattered page from his backpack and slowly handed it over to me. When I unfolded the paper, there were two lines written on the page: "So nice not to exist!" and "My life sucks." To unknowingly add salt to the wound, when randomly calling upon a number of students to read their lists aloud, the teacher chose him. He said he responded by saying, "I didn't write a list because I don't plan on getting married," at which point the teacher smiled at him, playfully poked him in the shoulder, and said, "Oh, that is what all boys your age say until they meet the right girl!" This teacher had not intentionally set out to make this student feel excluded and uncomfortable, yet this was surely the result. This is but one example among many of the heterosexism that LGBTQ youth experience each day.

What a difference it makes when sexual-minority youth *do* see their lives reflected in the world around them. One afternoon a former student, who had recently begun university, dropped by the school to see me. I had supported this young woman when she came out to family and friends in her final year of high school. She shared with me how good she felt when she stepped into the university centre for the first time and saw a big rainbow flag (symbolic of gay pride) with the words "Welcome" emblazoned on it. The flag was hanging over a desk strewn with literature advertising the LGBTQ group at the university. She said that although she had only been on campus for less than an hour, she experienced a feeling of "coming home." After she left my office, I sat wondering if there would ever be a day when LGBTQ students would step into Catholic schools and see such an inclusive symbol welcoming them. Would the day ever come when LGBTQ students would feel safe and at home in their schools? In that moment I recommitted myself to doing my part to ensure the answer will be "yes."

Homophobia can be a cruel by-product of heterosexism. Unfortunately, LGBTQ youth are exposed to homophobic statements many times daily. They sit in classrooms and walk through hallways where classmates randomly and recurrently use the statement "That's so gay!" as a euphuism for "That's so stupid." They watch as straight classmates tease each other, using the names fag or dyke, when they deem that a friend is sitting too close to a member of the same sex in the cafeteria or on the bus. They read hundreds of posted messages on their electronic devices, where most put-downs involve the use of hateful homophobic words. In hearing and reading the homophobic statements made to others around them, sexual-minority youth often fear for their own emotional and physical safety: "What would my peers say or do to me if they found out that *I* was gay?"

In a number of high schools homophobia is beginning to be discussed, but one of the areas very few high schools (Catholic or public) are addressing is transphobia, and how to support transgender students. It was twenty years ago when I became aware that one of my cousins was transgender. More recently, I have met and worked closely with a number of transgender students in my high school. Education has been crucial in enabling me to understand and support my cousin and these students. For this reason, I suggested to our school's PRISM (Pride and Respect for Individuals of a Sexual Minority) group that our focus for the next few years be on transgender education, with the goal of more fully supporting transgender students. Over the years our school had made great gains in building a school culture of kindness and care to support students, including lesbian and gay students, but we had not yet done education specific to transgender students. As in most high schools, our staff and students possessed minimal knowledge of the transgender experience.

Our PRISM group is blessed to have a transgender (male to female) student as part of its membership. For purposes of this discussion I will refer to this student as Erin. Erin has courageously decided to fully embrace who she is and to be out at school. She has been an invaluable contributor to our school's PRISM group by helping to educate all members, so that we may share our collective knowledge with the entire school community. The staff leader of PRISM and I decided that the first step in educating the school would be to educate the staff. It was for this reason that we asked Erin to consider speaking at one of our upcoming staff meetings. She was immediately up to the challenge. Several months later, Erin stood before us and unfolded the story of her life.

Erin told us that although she felt nervous speaking to a room full of teachers, it was important for her to do so, because the more we learned about transgender people the less time she would have to spend trying to help us understand her. Her words resonated with me. As a gay woman who is a daughter, sister, cousin, niece, aunt, friend, and colleague, at times I strive to help the heterosexual people in my life understand my lived experience. Taking the time to do this fosters understanding and empathy, but it can be tiring. As I sat there looking at Erin, I found myself imagining how emotionally exhausting it must be for her and other transgender persons, since most people around them know very little about the complexity of their daily lives.

As I listened to Erin speak, I was struck by a number of the insights she shared. She challenged the deeply embedded myth that physiology determines gender: that is, that if you have male genitalia then clearly you are male, and if you have female genitalia than clearly you are female. Referring to her male genitalia, she said, "This may be *what* I am, but being female is *who* I am." This simple statement drew an important distinction. She also spoke about the difference between gender identity and sexual orientation, noting that they are two distinct things although most people believe they are one and the same. She shared with us that she is frequently mistaken for a gay male even though she is a transgender female who identifies as heterosexual.

I was impressed by what Erin shared in her talk, and most striking to me was the overall tone of her presentation, which was hopeful and optimistic. Having endured much emotional stress in her young years, she exuded confidence and was resolute that her future would be bright. She spoke passionately about a number of personal goals she has set for herself, and shared that she wants her life to have purpose and meaning. This sense of purpose was reflected in her response to a staff member who asked, "In the future, do you want to be known as Erin the transgender person, or just as Erin?" She responded, "Neither, I want to be known as Erin, a person who made a difference in the world." What an incredible response from such a brave, courageous, and inspiring young woman!

Having worked to support a number of transgender students over the years, I have come to see that their lives are fraught with challenges, especially at school. Something as basic as using the washroom creates considerable tension for them. They struggle to find a bathroom and a change room (for participation in physical education classes) that enables them to feel safe and comfortable. They feel a level of discomfort when teachers use gender as a means of delegating tasks or dividing up students for group activities because it forces them to choose which side they should join. Transgender students feel awkward when they attend school dances and are made to choose between the male and female line in order to undergo the pat-down safety check required before entry.

Transgender students' legal names often cause them discomfort. Although all of the transgender students I have worked with have chosen to be known by a name reflective of the gender they identify as, most have not changed their name legally. In part, this is due to the laws of the province of Ontario that require a person to be eighteen years of age to legally change their name. Most high school students do not turn eighteen until their final year; some do not reach this age until after graduation. The result is that transgender students' legal names are the ones appearing on teacher class lists, and are the names most often used. When a transgender student's legal name is read aloud in class and used by a teacher (reflecting the gender opposite to the one the student identifies as), it creates anxiety and embarrassment. These are but a few examples of the number of uncomfortable predicaments transgender students find themselves in at school.

Most recently, I supported Erin in her desire to play on our school's senior girls' basketball team. I was dismayed to learn that it was a requirement of our board's athletic policy (and, I am guessing, other school boards' athletic policies as well) that medical documentation be produced to prove she had been transitioning for at least one year. I am aware that Erin is not the first student to be asked to seek approval to play a sport in our school. Students who move from school to school within the same jurisdiction also require an approval process. In the case of those students, however, the approval needed is due to external circumstances and is unrelated to who the student is as a person. Erin's situation is different: she was being asked to seek approval for simply being who she was.

I cannot tell you how awkward, disconcerting, and sad it felt to sit across from Erin's mother and explain the requirements needing to be met in order for her child to receive approval to play basketball. I knew that Erin's mother had already faced many challenges raising and loving a transgender child. It felt terrible to be asking her to negotiate yet another hurdle. What stayed with me most from our conversation was her response when I apologized to her for having to ask her to manage yet another obstacle. She looked over at me, and with a comforting voice said, "It's okay." I felt both angry and sad that any parents should have to resign themselves to meeting requirements so that their child may enjoy the same basic rights other parents can take for granted for their children. I would surmise that the athletic committee's upholding of this policy was an attempt to ensure fairness, but I struggled with how fair it was to demand that the mother of a transgender student produce medical documentation in order for her child to be allowed to play on a sports team — something no other parent has to do.

Throughout the process of working closely with Erin and her mother, many questions gnawed at me, not just at an intellectual level, but at the level of the soul: Who are we to make this young woman and her family jump through hoops so she can play on a high school basketball team, simply because she is transgender? I struggled with the expectation that transgender students must be in the process of transitioning in order to be approved. What about transgender students who do not believe they need to change their physiology to be who they are, and instead challenge us to broaden our understanding of gender and what constitutes being male and female? Under the present athletic committee policy, these transgender persons would be completely forbidden to play. Is this not in violation of their human rights?

I felt there was discrepancy in the policy. The policy required documented medical proof that male to female transgender students be in the process of transitioning, but did not ask young people transitioning from female to male to do the same. Is the assumption that male to female transgender persons will be bigger and stronger, which will give their team an unfair advantage? If so, this generalization should not be presumed. I am sure there are some male to female transgender students who are physically smaller than other females. Even if they are stronger, is the overriding goal of participation on a high school team to win, or to give *every* young person the opportunity to participate, feel a sense of belonging, and learn important life lessons from working together as team? I know some highly competitive individuals will disagree, but I maintain that competition and the desire to win should not override the right for *all* kids to participate and enjoy high school athletics.

Perhaps safety is the overall concern. Based on the false assumption that a male to female transgender person will always be stronger than a non-transgender female, is there a concern that they will pose a safety risk by overpowering or hurting a member of the other team? I have seen a number of incredibly strong women playing on high school sports teams, and I am guessing that at times their coaches have asked them to be cognizant of their size when competing against smaller opponents. When a transgender student does happen to be physically bigger and stronger than other players, why need it be any different for them? There will, certainly, be special concerns that must be addressed when a team has a transgender player. For example, there will need to be a safe and comfortable place provided for them to change in before and after the game. At school we work to ensure alternative arrangements are provided for transgender students, so we would simply need to do the same in this situation.

I recognize that meeting the needs of transgender students is new territory for most schools, and therefore, growing pains are to be expected. I have experienced those growing pains first-hand in working with these students. I feel strongly, however, that in establishing and enacting policies for transgender students, we remember first and foremost that we are talking about *human beings*, not issues. We must always act sensitively, compassionately, and humbly, and never ever compromise the integrity, dignity, and core spirit of transgender persons in the process of our stumbling.

It is vital that the adults in the lives of LBGTQ students "have their back" and support them, because some of their peers can be hard-hearted and merciless. It is a sad reality that many sexual-minority students become targets for the darts of ignorance and fear stored in the teenage arsenal. Study after study indicates that an overwhelming majority of LGBTQ students have experienced bullying due to their sexual orientation. They are frequently harassed simply for being who they are. Mean-spirited classmates make the lives of some of these students such living hell that significant numbers of them drop out of school. Some turn to drugs and self-harm to try to numb out. Many LGBTQ students become depressed, and sadly, some take their lives as a way of seeking relief from the cruelty and pain that sears their soul. With homophobia, and transphobia surrounding them, is it any wonder that many sexual-minority youth feel unwanted, alone, and scared? It is no coincidence that Ellen DeGeneres, a popular daytime TV host who identifies as gay, ends every show with, "Be kind to one another." She knows full well, as do most sexual-minority persons, what *un*-kind sounds and feels like. Sadly, sexual-minority youth know un-kind all too well.

To further LGBTQ students' feelings of isolation, many of them feel they have no one to turn to. Unlike students of a racial minority, who for the most part feel free to talk to their parents about the racial slurs or stereotypes they have experienced, these young people generally do not turn to their parents when experiencing difficulties, fearing the negative repercussions of coming out to them. They do not turn to close friends, for the same reason. Having to live with and carry around a secret contributes to the isolation and alienation many LGBTQ youth feel.

As I said above, depression is a reality for many sexual-minority youth. A period of depression often occurs before they arrive at a place of self-acceptance. Sometimes the depression is linked to self-loathing stemming from internalized homophobia — when a gay person comes to believe, on the inside, the negative things that are said to and about them on the outside. One of the biggest tasks in working with LGBTQ students is helping them unpack and unlearn the negative feelings they have come to accept about themselves. In helping them address the homophobia and transphobia found both in the world around them and within themselves, they are able to move from a place of self-loathing to a place of self-acceptance, and celebrate who they are. Self-celebration is a lifelong process for sexual-minority teens, and will continue to be until the outside world becomes more accepting and supportive of them. Ongoing education is paramount to building communities where LGBTQ students feel welcomed, supported, and loved.

WALKING A TIGHT ROPE

As an educator who has worked in a Catholic school board for over thirty years, I know that there is the need for more people to advocate for LGBTQ students. Many staff help in their own subtle ways, but more Catholic educators need to speak up publicly on behalf of sexual-minority students, because historically, with the exception of the quiet work of a few staff members, these students have been left to fend for themselves. It is fair to say that these youth are still invisible in most Catholic schools, and supporting them continues to be a huge area of need.

Sexual-minority students motivate me to want to make a difference. They ground me and inspire me, and are the reason I stay and work in the Catholic system, as increasingly difficult as that decision has proven to be for me both personally and professionally. Their struggles and stories compel and challenge me, and serve to deepen my commitment to ensuring they are given the voice they need and deserve. When I get frustrated and angry at the official Catholic teachings about homosexuality, which make it difficult for me to feel free to be open about who I am, it is the faces of LGBTQ youth that I see and their presence I feel. Their courage and inner strength help me continue to fight passionately for positive change on their behalf.

In this past decade there has been reason for hope. In 2009 the Ministry of Education (Ontario) released an *Equity and Inclusion Policy* that mandates that all schools must ensure every student is treated equitably and feels safe at school. One of the groups specifically named in the document is LGBTQ youth. In 2012, on the heels of the *Equity and Inclusion Policy*, came the *Accepting Schools Act* (Bill13) mandating that all publicly funded schools in Ontario provide support for sexual-minority youth. The government identified GSA (Gay Straight Alliance) groups as an important way to offer such support. This was significant because with the release of this legislation, Catholic schools, which are publicly funded in Ontario, could no longer opt out of ensuring supports were in place for LGBTQ students.

As I write this, Catholic school boards in Ontario are preparing to put supports in place for sexual-minority youth in a more systematized way. The increased supports that will be put in place have been a long time in coming, so there is cause for celebration. Disappointing to me, however, is that the initiative did not emanate from Catholic boards themselves, based on a vision of inclusion and justice for all, but evolved in response to the political pressure put on them by the Ministry of Education and the provincial government. The Catholic Church has a rich history of social-justice teaching, which seeks to ensure that the dignity and rights of all people are preserved and protected. It saddens me that Ontario Catholic school boards are finally moving in the direction of putting formal supports in place for LGBTQ youth, not out of an inherent sense of social justice, but in response to outside political pressure.

The 2012 mandate by the provincial government was welcome news not only for sexual-minority students, but also for those of us working to support these students in Catholic schools. The government, in providing the mandatory legislation, allowed us to do what we knew in our hearts needed to be done a long, long time ago. Now *all* Catholic school boards had no option but to swing the closet doors open and provide more formalized supports for gay, lesbian, bisexual and transgender students.

It is important to acknowledge that before this moment in time, there were people in Catholic schools supporting LGBTQ youth. In the Catholic school board where I am employed, there were pockets of passionate and deeply committed Catholic educators quietly supporting LGBTQ youth for many years. As one of those educators, I would best describe our shared experience as one of walking a political tight rope, as we strove to balance what we knew needed to be done to support LGBTQ students with trying to avoid the attention and criticism of other staff members, parents, senior administrators, and Church officials, who might take offence with what we were doing to help these kids. We desperately wanted to do more for our students, but at that time no official permission had been granted to do so. People occupying senior administrative positions were navigating their own tight ropes. Fear reigned supreme. Some senior administrators were acutely aware of what needed to be done to support sexual-minority students, and felt deep compassion for them, but their resolve to take action was paralyzed by the fact that Catholic Church authorities were not overtly supportive of work being done in this area. Before the legislation, the senior administration's means of providing support was to turn a blind eye to the quiet work being done. Although on board, some senior administrators feared calling attention to the support being offered to LGBTQ students, due to the scrutiny they feared it might invite. Although their turning a blind eye helped the important work to continue, this approach did little to increase the visible supports needed so that more vulnerable kids could be reached and helped. What resulted in my board were many years where only a handful of passionate, committed educators (dispersed among several high schools) were trying to support the significant numbers of LGBTQ kids coming off the rails daily. What haunted those of us in the trenches was the knowledge that there were so many kids out there not getting any support whatsoever. Without permission from senior administration to develop specific groups to meet the needs of LGBTQ youth, we had no way of reaching all of the sexual-minority students in our schools, so their needs went unmet.

From the mid 1980's up until Bill 13 was passed in 2012, I would sporadically write to senior administrators and trustees identifying the urgent need to get further supports in place. I would clearly state that the little pockets of care we had in our schools were not nearly enough. Most of my correspondence would go unanswered. The lack of response was not due to my advocacy falling on deaf ears or uncaring hearts, I knew many of the people I was writing to, and had seen from personal experience that they were good people who genuinely cared about kids. They felt caught in a bind and, as I said, were walking their own tight ropes. I think they feared backlash from some parents and Church officials, if they stuck their necks out and allowed those of us in the trenches to support LGBTQ students in more formalized ways. I truly believe it was this paralyzing fear that kept Catholic leaders positioned firmly in place, and that explained why they refrained from speaking out publicly about the need to support sexual-minority youth. Without the tacit support of Catholic ecclesial authorities, senior administrators felt their hands were tied.

It was a stressful and difficult time. No systematized supports were in place, and LGBTQ kids were self-destructing; they were cutting themselves, starving themselves, numbing out through drug use, running away from home, battling chronic depression, and making attempts on their lives. As a person supporting them, I found myself sitting in a profoundly humbling place. They were opening their hearts and unfolding their lives before me, entrusting me with their anguish and pain. The threads of their stories were far too similar. Rejection, isolation, alienation. "No one even knows I am here. I am just a nobody," said one young man to me through his sobbing. And sadly, in our schools it was easy to see why he felt this way. He really *was* invisible. When you witness such despondency and emotional carnage, you feel compelled to act. It has been said that all it takes for evil to persist is for good people to do nothing. This statement is incredibly challenging, and haunts me in the healthiest of ways, as a strong call to action.

Over the past several decades I have delivered many workshops on the need for supports for LGBTQ youth in Catholic schools. Many of these workshops have taken place at provincial conferences. In my interactions with Catholic educators across the province, it has become glaringly apparent to me that many Catholic school boards clearly saw the need for supports, but were afraid to be the first board to risk taking the first step. In mandating the existence of groups to support LGBTQ students in all schools, the provincial government lifted the pressure off Catholic school boards. Now, no Catholic board would need to risk going first.

As I stated earlier, I will always feel saddened by the fact that it took outside political pressure to get some Catholic school boards to do what was the right thing to do all along. In baptism, Catholics are anointed *priest, prophet, and king,* and part of the prophetic mission of that baptismal call is to do what needs to be done to uphold the dignity and respect of *all* people. I clearly understand the power of fear, and totally appreciate the debilitating hold it can have on people, otherwise, why would I not be totally out as a gay person at work right now? Having said this, I will always question why Catholic school systems that are called to exemplify the values of Jesus turned their backs on some of their most vulnerable for so long. It is upsetting to me that Catholic boards, as a collective, did not stand together in solidarity and say, "Our LGBTQ kids desperately need our help, and we are going to get on with what needs to be done to support and save them!" — then, in a spirit of doing what needed to be done for their own, have the courage to stand up to Church authorities, if required.

After the province of Ontario mandated that all publicly funded schools have supports in place for LGBTQ youth, the Ontario Catholic Trustees' Association, along with the Institute for Catholic Education and the Ontario Catholic bishops, said they would adhere to the legislation, but that support groups in Catholic schools would have to be consistent with Catholic teaching, and as such, would not be called Gay-Straight Alliances (GSA). I am unsure why the name GSA was suspect.

In the media, some Catholic trustees across the province voiced concern that gay students in public schools used GSA groups to meet other gay students for dating purposes. I heard the term "gay propaganda" frequently used in discussions about GSA groups. In one newspaper article, a Catholic trustee commented that teens are easily influenced and can't possibly know they are gay at such a young age. He voiced his concern that GSA groups might pressure some students to become gay. At this point I was quite curious what benefits he surmised would come with teens "choosing" to be gay. The gay teens I work with struggle daily to accept themselves due to the homophobia around them, which shows itself in heterosexist comments, homophobic jokes, harassment, and bullying — all of which leave many of them feeling ashamed, conflicted, lonely, and depressed. I am not seeing the benefits any teenager would find in *choosing* to be gay! I was struck time and time again by the level of ignorance in these GSA-related discussions, and thought to myself that the people struggling with the development of GSA groups would be the ones who would benefit most from taking part in them. It would allow them to become more informed concerning these issues, and to move beyond the ignorance and misguided myths reflected in many of their statements and judgments.

The Catholic response (via the Ontario Catholic School Trustees' Association, the Institute for Catholic Education, and the Ontario Catholic bishops) to the government's mandate was to state that a Catholic framework would be provided, consistent with Catholic teaching, to direct Catholic schools regarding what the groups would be named and what they would look like. The framework was promised by the fall after the legislation was released, but did not arrive until half a year later. It struck me, on more than one occasion, that while bishops and other Catholic stakeholders were deliberating around tables for months over what the groups should be named (to ensure the groups would stay Catholic), gay kids in Catholic schools across the province continued — in rates three times higher than those for heterosexual youth — to drop out, deal with depression, get high, experience emotional and physical abuse at home and/or at school, be bullied, cut themselves, make attempts on their own lives, and in some cases take their own lives.

When the framework was finally released, the name it suggested be used in place of GSA was "Respecting Difference." Personally, I did not care what name was chosen. What was most important to me was that the groups get up and running so students could be supported. Having said that, I am not convinced that including the word "difference" in the name was the best way to help LGBTQ youth feel welcome and part of their school communities!

Not long after the Catholic trustees released their framework, a colleague (whom I work alongside to run groups to support LGBTQ youth in our high school) and I were approached by a journalist from a local newspaper to do an interview about the sexual-minority support groups we had in place. We spent time together discerning whether we should grant the interview, because we did not want to be thrust into the political debate. Our core intent for starting a formalized group in our school was to support LGBTQ kids, not to make a political statement. We worried that in sharing our proactive ideas and talking about the supports we had in place, we might inadvertently cause a stir in an already highly sensitized political climate, and in this way endanger the good work we had been doing to take care of our students. But we also knew the benefits of doing the interview. The work we had been doing in this area at our school was ahead of the work being done at most other Catholic high schools across the province. We believed it could benefit other Catholic high schools to see that there was a high school already doing work explicitly in support of LGBTQ students, and would perhaps pave the way for them to do the same. We also felt that a newspaper article would give us the opportunity to make more of our sexual-minority students aware of the supports we had in place at our school, and assure them of our commitment to their safety.

On a personal level, I had to decide whether or not, yet again, I was willing to speak from the stance of an "objective" voice (as I had felt forced to do in my written response to the homosexuality document mentioned earlier). I knew if I agreed to do the interview, I would not be able to do it honestly and openly from the perspective of a gay educator in a Catholic school. After much dialogue and reflection, my colleague and I agreed to be interviewed. The interview lasted two hours, and by the end we were exhausted. We had expended much energy picking our words with caution; there was the need to balance what we wanted to share, openly and honestly, with what we felt our board would be comfortable with. Many times throughout the interview we wanted to be more honest. At one point the interviewer asked if we ever got frustrated at how slow moving and stuck the Catholic Church seems to be around this issue. I wanted to stand up and respond with a resounding "Yes!" but instead, smiled in her direction. Neither my colleague nor I are shy about pushing the envelope, but we did not want to put ourselves in a situation where all the good things we had worked hard to put in place would be shut down and prevented from moving forward. This was a real possibility if we said too much to the press and received backlash for doing so. I was extremely careful in selecting my words so as not to reveal my identity as a gay woman. Again, I felt forced to swallow my integrity by staying closeted. It is difficult to find words to describe what it feels like to have to defy your own soul in this way. It feels like you are turning your back on yourself. I know few feelings that are as formidable. After the interview, it struck me that over the years I had seemed to spend an awful lot of time walking a tight rope. But, at least this time I had a courageous friend and colleague bravely walking the rope with me!

Around this time, a superintendent and I were talking about an upcoming anti-homophobia event that our school's sexual-minority support group was organizing to further educate our school community. The superintendent suggested that we move cautiously and pay attention to the optics when planning any anti-homophobia event. He cautioned us against doing anything that might invoke the suspicion that we have a *gay agenda* at our school. I like the term *gay agenda* about as much as I like the word *tolerance* — it is my belief that people are to be accepted, honoured, and celebrated, not just tolerated. When I hear the term *gay agenda* I am never really sure what it actually means. I think it might have something to do with the misguided notion that a gay person can influence a heterosexual person to turn gay by pushing some type of *agenda* on him or her. As gay people we are powerful, but not that powerful! If, as an educator, my fight to ensure LGBTQ youth feel safe and wanted and are protected from undue emotional anguish is an "agenda," then yes, admittedly I have a clear *gay agenda* and make no apologies for it.

As I mentioned earlier, the Equity and Inclusion legislation opened doors for Catholic school boards to do more explicit work in supporting LGBTQ students. Around this same time, I was invited to be part of a board-wide working committee whose mandate was to get supports in place for sexual-minority students in all of our schools. As I sat at the first committee meeting I was struck by how many years (truth be known, decades) it had taken our board to get to this point. But at least we had arrived there, many Catholic boards had not - I am proud to say that my board is one of the lead Catholic boards doing this work in the province.

At our first meeting I suggested that it would be important to have gay voices around the table, and offered to ask a few of my gay educational colleagues who had moved to the public board to come and take part in our dialogue. Although I knew the committee would probably find this recommendation too controversial, I still felt it was important to put the suggestion forward as a reminder that gay people need to be invited to speak *for themselves*. As I attended committee meetings, I found it increasingly difficult to offer input posing as a heterosexual person. There were things I needed to be able to bring forward and name from the perspective of a gay person.

Gay people generally test the waters before coming out to those around them. It is about trying to "get a read" on people in order to try to determine how safe it will be to come forward and be honest about who we are. It is like developing something akin to a sixth sense. This is something I do when interacting with new people and finding myself in new situations. I am always hyper-vigilant in observing my surroundings, constantly evaluating if I am with a group that will judge or accept me. This directs how honest and open I will be about my life with the people I am around. It takes a lot of energy.

Several years into my involvement on the board-wide committee, focused on supporting LGBTQ youth, it was this "sixth sense" that I used to risk coming out to fellow committee members. Earlier that month I had come out to all secondary administrators at a committee meeting. Although I had come out to a number of individual colleagues over the years, this was the first time I was publicly identifying myself as a gay person in a Catholic professional setting. Both groups received me with care, reverence, and respect. This did not surprise me, given the compassionate human beings I knew them to be. These colleagues seemed to understand and appreciate the difficult position I found myself in, being a gay woman working in a Catholic school board. Coming out to these two groups brought an inner freedom I had not experienced previously in my professional life. Despite my elation, however, sadness and frustration still remained, since I still did not feel free to be completely out at work, among students and colleagues.

CHALLENGE AND HOPE

Sometimes I shake my head about the fact that it is the twenty-first century and I still have to concern myself with being authentically who I am at work, simply because I am gay. Many of the LGBTQ youth I work with have figured out that I am gay (there really is such a thing as *gaydar!*), and so I worry about the impact my staying closeted has on them. I struggle with the message I may be sending. Am I giving them the impression that gay people need to stay in closets and apologize for who they are? Am I being hypocritical in challenging them to accept and celebrate who they are, while I remain closeted at work? I wish I could be totally upfront and honest with them about who I am. There are days I tell myself I am done with living a double life, and flirt with throwing caution to the wind and completely coming out. What holds me back is the fear of the consequences that could result. Would there be backlash from parents who believe that a gay administrator working in a Catholic school is unacceptable? Could this possibly put pressure on my board and result in my being removed from my high school, impacting my ability to support the LGBTQ youth I work with daily? Even if coming out to staff and students did not entail the loss of my role as a vice-principal, would my personal life be put under close scrutiny? If so, this would feel incredibly invasive. I fear that coming out while still working in a Catholic school would render me vulnerable to the hateful projections of people who deem being gay an abomination. In the year 2000 I attended a human rights rally in Washington, and had enough "God hates fags!" and "Gays rot in hell!" signs pushed in my face to remove any illusion that all professing Christians are accepting!

This coming spring will mark the end of my career as a Catholic educator. I look with anticipation and excitement to being able to live my life openly and freely for the first time. It saddens me that I will be age fifty-four before experiencing that freedom, but I take full responsibility for the choices I have made. I could have left the Catholic school system, but I consciously chose to stay. I am aware that in retirement I will not be totally free, because inner freedom is difficult to attain no matter who you are, gay or otherwise. All human beings are held captive at some level, but I will certainly welcome a fuller taste of freedom!

I am not naïve. I know that once out of the Catholic system, I will still need to deal with the homophobia that exists in the world, and it is my intent to work toward its eradication whenever and wherever I see it. I will never retire from supporting LGBTQ youth, nor do I foresee a time in my life where I will. Having said that, it is my sincerest of hopes that, sooner rather than later, advocacy for LGBTQ youth will be unnecessary because sexual-minority teens will feel welcomed and celebrated alongside heterosexual youth — in their families, in their schools, and in their religious institutions.

It is also my hope that one day lesbian, gay, bisexual, and transgender Catholic educators will feel welcome, safe, and secure. The Church's teaching that gay relationships are intrinsically disordered disallows them from being open in sharing who they are. In retirement I will be in a safer position to advocate more explicitly for their needs. LGBTQ educators should never be made to feel less than who they are, or have to hide and apologize for who they are and who they love. Some LGBTQ Catholic educators, through the grace of God, have quietly managed to find each other to offer mutual support, but they should not have to live with a secret. *All* teachers should have the freedom to be open and honest about who they are and who they love.

Catholic school boards would benefit greatly from having LGBTQ educators out and visible. Research strongly indicates that the mental health of sexual-minority youth is vastly improved when they have openly gay, lesbian, bisexual and transgender persons they can go to for direction and support. LGBTQ educators would serve as vital role models for students and would provide them with much needed encouragement and care. It is an understatement to call it *unfortunate* that Catholic teachers of a sexual minority are unable to be out and available as positive role models for youth in Catholic schools. I know how important it was for my coming-out process to have gay people close by who understood my experience and who encouraged and supported me. Accepting and celebrating LGBTQ Catholic educators would go a long way to ensuring sexual-minority students are extended kindness and treated equitably.

I have not been subtle here in sharing my feelings about the Catholic Church's official teaching about homosexuality, and the impact it has on LGBTQ persons. It is for reasons of personal integrity that I have been forthright and honest in naming my hurt and anger. I have been totally honest, in hopes that change can happen so that the future will be more loving and inclusive for LGBTQ persons. After all, if a reality is not named, how can it be addressed?

Church teachings about homosexuality have profoundly affected how I, and other gay persons, have been made to feel about ourselves; and they have limited the supports desperately needed in Catholic schools to help youth. It is upsetting to me how the institutional Church has oppressed and hurt, not only me, but many LGBTQ persons. It is my firm belief that because God created persons to be relational — to express and receive love - it is wrong to tell gay persons that it is a moral imperative that they live celibate lives and not enjoy the beauty of committed intimate relationships. The Catholic Church's official teaching about homosexual relationships contributes to the unhealthy attitudes people have about gay persons, and serves to legitimize homophobia in all its hateful forms and expression.

My experience with the Catholic Church as the *people of God* (as wonderfully laid out in the documents of Vatican II) has been qualitatively different from my experience of the institutional Church and its official teachings about homosexuality. I have received love and affirmation by many Catholic educational colleagues and friends, who have consistently supported me as a person and as a professional. My distress and criticism is not with the Church as the *people of God,* but with the institutional Church and its official teachings about homosexuality, for it is these teachings, and their interpretations, that have served to categorize, judge, isolate, and hurt gay people. It is these teachings that have held Catholic school boards captive, limiting what they can do explicitly to support LGBTQ students and staff.

I do not believe that anyone or anything, the institutional Church included, is all good or all bad. I respect a number of the stances the official Catholic Church has taken, particularly its preferential option for the poor (that preference be given to the powerless in society, including the poor), which serves as a prophetic voice desperately needed in the world. The good work the Catholic Church does, however, should not render it exempt from healthy criticism and from being challenged to grow in significant areas that need addressing.

I am thankful that I was raised within a religious tradition, and I am grateful to Catholicism for introducing me to a sense of the sacred from a very early age. The seeds of my adult spirituality, which I supremely value and honour, were sown during my childhood, and I am thankful for this precious gift. Yet this same religious tradition taught me and other gay persons to deny who we are, and in doing so contributed to feelings of inferiority and shame. I believe this is why many gay people are overachievers. It is an attempt to *earn* the love of others: if I am really good at something then perhaps others will overlook this "sinful thing" about me and still like me. Sadly, the self-loathing caused in part by Church teachings about homosexuality has propelled some gay Catholics to utter despair, even to the point of taking their own lives.

The Church's refusal to validate gay relationships has a strong impact on gay Catholics. It sends a strong message that who and how they love is sinful, which makes them feel shame about themselves. It is my prayer that the Church will do its much-needed work in this area in order to cease doing emotional damage to sexual-minority persons, especially to vulnerable sexual-minority youth.

It is true that Catholic school boards are now freer to do the work that needs to be done to support *all* youth, but this freedom remains limited as long as the Catholic Church continues to teach what it does about homosexual relationships. A priest recently told me he believes my interpretation of the contemporary Church's approach to the issue of homosexuality is stuck in the Middle Ages. He argued that the Catholic Church *is* pastoral and sensitive to gay persons. If this is the case, where are all the out gay priests? Would gay priests not feel free and safe to be openly gay if, as this priest suggests, the Church is so accepting?

In the teaching of the Catholic Church, there is still no room for gay relationships. The Church continues to compartmentalize gay persons by separating who they are (*it is okay to be gay*) from how they express themselves (*same-sex physical expression is intrinsically disordered*). This is not how gay people experience themselves. For gay persons, no different than for heterosexual persons, sexual expression is the outward expression of who they have come to know and experience themselves to be on the inside. It is natural and beautiful to want to express one's love through physical intimacy, no matter what one's sexual orientation.

I have worked alongside, been spiritually formed by, and continue to have deep appreciation for a number of Catholic clergymen who are men of abiding faith. They have deep compassion for gay persons and for their relationships, but sadly, they fear going public with their support of sexual-minority persons and gay unions. I have priest friends who are gay and who, like me, feel forced to be secretive and silent about who they are. It saddens me that the institutional Church does not provide freedom, even for its own.

In order to be true to this chapter's title, *The Path of Integrity*, I have made the choice to name the reality of my lived experience — the good, the bad, and yes, even the ugly. Although I will always be grateful for the spiritual worldview given me by the Catholic Church, it is important for me to name that this same Church has been the source of much hurt in my life. Its teachings about homosexual relationships have caused much heartache. No one should be asked to apologize for who they are and how they love. I believe the Church needs to understand that when you tell LGBTQ persons their love is wrong, you are saying that God has made an error, because God made them as they are. I feel it would be a total dishonouring of God's creation to not follow *the path of integrity* and be who I truly am.

The process of discovering who I am as a gay woman and the struggle to maintain integrity while working within a Catholic school system (which must uphold the official teachings of the Church, including its teachings about homosexuality) has proven to be immeasurably challenging.

Perhaps that is why I have found myself drawn time and time again to a line from a Bruce Cockburn song that states, "Nothing worth having comes without some kind of fight. Got to kick at the darkness 'til it bleeds daylight." This lyric inspires me because it is a reminder that integrity is *always* worth the fight, even when the road is arduous and long, and exacts a cost. Cockburn's words are a hope-filled promise that over time the fight will be worth it, and daylight will indeed come!

In striving to walk *the path of integrity* I have had to make distinct and defining choices along the way, and accept the consequences of those choices at every turn. Walking *the path of integrity* has not been the easiest route — it never is — but I believe it is the only path that leads us to our truth, enables us to touch the divine within, and ultimately brings us freedom.

I have heard it said that God hates people like me for who I am, for my "sinful lifestyle." But today I told God I was gay and God wasn't shocked or angered, or judgmental or cruel. In fact, God held me in warm embrace and said: "[Joan], you are precious in my sight… and I love you." (Isaiah 43:4)

Deepening Your Life…

How do you define personal integrity? Is integrity a value that is important to you?

Has there ever been a time when your personal integrity was challenged, or even threatened? How did you feel? How did you respond?

What is one value you live your life by that you feel is worth fighting to protect and maintain? Why is this value of such importance to you?

In your opinion, what are some characteristics of people who are free? On a personal level, what do you need to do or let go of in order to experience greater inner freedom?

Do you feel you live your life as you desire, or is a big part of your life lived to please others? If you live to please others, how does this make you feel? What do you need to do to take back your life?

What are you more conscious about doing in your life today than you were five to ten years ago?

Have you ever let pressure from the outside keep you from doing something you felt called to do on the inside? How did it feel to let the outside pressure win?

Have you ever shared information with a loved one that you knew could cause disappointment, rejection, or the loss of their love? Knowing the cost it could exact, why did you still choose to share this information?

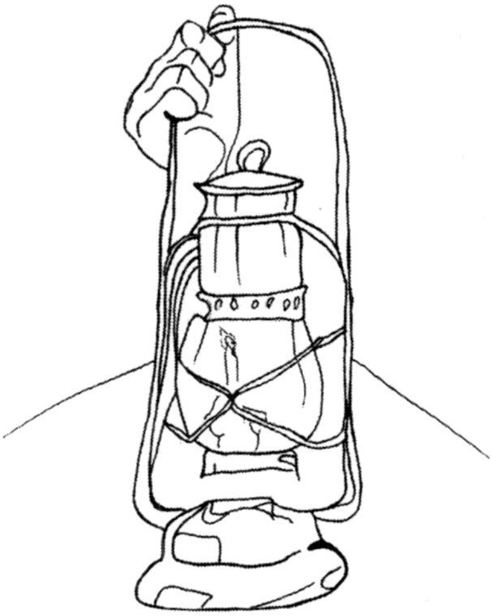

CHAPTER THREE

Guided by Grace

GOD IS NEAR

Over the years I have read many insightful and inspiring books dedicated to the search for God. Many of these texts have provided details on how to meditate and pray in order to have a personal experience of God. The premise is that if we learn to be quiet and still, we will hear the voice of God. Although I have undoubtedly benefited from reading such texts, over time I have come to understand, and know deeply, that you really do not have to search for the Divine at all. I have discovered that in as much as I have searched for God, God has searched for me, and I have come to understand that God longs for us and continually creates opportunities to be felt and known.

One of the ways God has found me is through gracing my life with *spirit guides*; mentors who have helped direct my life at key times. These *spirit guides* have been authentic witnesses of faith in very unassuming ways. Their vision, integrity, compassion, and conviction have fuelled the lamp that has lit the path ahead. They have given me the courage and faith to take important steps forward. It is my belief that God graced me with *spirit guides* to draw me close, move me toward greater consciousness, and deepen my life. I have been blessed with many *spirit guides*, and to honour each would require a book unto itself, but I highlight here a few who have been pivotal in directing my spiritual path.

Previous chapters elucidated the key role my parents played in my formation as a person. This formation extended into my spiritual life. My parents were my earliest *spirit guides* as they shared and witnessed their belief in God, and ensured I was raised with a sense of the sacred. They played a foundational role in my spiritual journey and encouraged me to keep God as a close and trusted companion. The early seeds of faith they planted, along with the safe and trusting environment they provided, created an openness in me that allowed me to be receptive to others and learn from them as I moved forward in the world. Without the love and support given me by my parents, I would never have possessed the ability to experience the divine within, because I would never have felt worthy of such a divine visit. I will be forever grateful for the sacred gifts of faith and love that my parents generously gave to me that enabled me to feel worthy of love.

At age twelve I came to meet the first significant *spirit guide* outside my family system. Her name was Sister Perpetua, and she was my grade seven teacher. On the first day of school she walked into the classroom dressed in black and white from head to toe, carrying herself calmly and with confidence. I remember eyeing up the larger-than-life wooden rosary that hung limply from her left hip, and wondering if there was any truth behind the stories my mother had told about "the early days" in her school, where nuns rapped the knuckles of misbehaving students with their prayer beads. I was not a child who got into a lot of trouble, but I did have my moments, so I was quite eager to know what Sr. Perpetua's rosary was and was not used for!

My classmates and I had never had a nun for a teacher so we were quite curious, and a bit tentative. It did not take long, however, for this effervescent nun to win us over. Sister

Perpetua had a sparkle in her eye and a fire in her heart. Her enthusiasm was endearing and we responded quickly to her. She had a keen interest in getting to know each of us on a personal level, so our initial class discussions were about our lives and what mattered most to us. Sr. Perpetua shared a bit of her background with us, and we came to discover that she had great love for the aboriginal children she had taught in previous years. Her keen interest in them gave us the impression that it would not be long before she loved us too! As she shared her many stories, it became obvious to me that she would teach our class lessons far exceeding those contained in any textbook. My initial instincts would prove true; we would come to learn much from this impassioned nun.

From the outset I loved Sr. Perpetua's spunk and joie de vivre. Her passion was incredibly magnetic, drawing us all in. I can still picture her running out to the baseball diamond alongside us at gym time. Not one to watch life from the sidelines, Sr. Perpetua always joined in the game. She would run to the outfield, plant her feet firmly in the grass, and hoist her black robe up to just above her knees, so she could squat and ready herself to catch any balls that might reach right field. Smacking her right fist into her glove, she'd bellow out "C'mon batter, put it right here!" Everyone in the class thoroughly enjoyed her and without exception agreed she was really cool, especially for a nun.

Sister Perpetua was genuine and alive, and for this reason I quickly grew to love and respect her. I do not remember many details about the academic lessons she taught, but I do remember the caring and supportive way she consistently treated us. I particularly recall the ease with which she laughed alongside us, which made it easy for us to relate to her and place our trust in her. As a young girl, self-conscious as any prepubescent, I somehow did not mind the times she would tease me. This happened most often when I would get frustrated with math. If I did not understand how to do a particular question, I had a habit of putting my pencil down on the desk and scrunching up my nose to create a look of utter disdain and disgust. Sister Perpetua would quickly pick up on my frustration and instead of responding by chastising me, she would walk over to me, lean over my desk, get right in my face, and mimic me by scrunching up *her* nose. She would hold this position until I laughed, and only after she had cajoled me out of my frustrated state would she help me with the question at hand. Sr. Perpetua was not one to lord authority over people. She humbly walked alongside us, all the time encouraging us to come to recognize and celebrate the capabilities we possessed within.

One of the most significant memories I have from being a student in Sister Perpetua's class is the image of her praying. She would teach us prayers, many of which I had not previously heard. I struggled to understand the meaning of them because the language was foreign to me. Words like "beseech" and "immaculate" were not words I had ever heard, let alone used or understood, but what I did understand was how sincerely Sister Perpetua prayed those words. That is what stayed with me. What was abundantly clear was that the woman praying before me shared a genuine intimacy with God. It was apparent that Sr. Perpetua and God shared a relationship that was real, palpable, and strong. I remember harbouring the hope that one day I too could share this type of close relationship with God. It is only now, many years later, that I truly appreciate what a profound and significant gift Sister Perpetua gave me in showing that God is not a concept, but a real, felt presence. I am thankful for learning early in life that God isn't distant or someone you have to work hard to find, but is an abiding presence as close as your next breath.

It is rather interesting that I do not recall Sr. Perpetua speaking directly about God much at all, but the way she prayed, and the compassionate and nurturing way she treated us, gave me the impression that God was always present, not elusive or someone you had to seek. God was someone you simply had to acknowledge and let in. What a precious spiritual gem to be given at such a young age, the understanding that God lives within, around, and through you. The witness of Sr. Perpetua's faith taught me that intimacy with God is more than possible, because God is always near. She also taught me that God is in our hearts for a reason, so that we might put faith and love into action. Sr. Perpetua believed that we are called to live compassionately, by encouraging each other and caring for one another. She modelled this through example, by how deeply she cared for us.

Teaching a large class did not deter Sister Perpetua from taking time to get to know us as individuals. She seemed to enjoy nurturing our unique talents. I still smile today as I think about the musical band she pulled together in my grade seven year. Somehow she knew I played the accordion, so she gathered me and three other musical students from class, to form a band she called *Sister Perpetua's Yippees!* Like a proud mother she premiered our band at a school concert. I must have *really* liked her in order to be willing to go up on stage and play my accordion, given that I had been a closet accordionist up until that time! That year, my mother had undergone kidney surgery, which resulted in her being hospitalized for an extended period of time. Sr. Perpetua knew I was very close to my mom and intuited how deeply worried I was about her, so she was extra attentive and supportive of me during those difficult weeks. I can't help but wonder if *Sister Perpetua's Yippees* wasn't, at least to some degree, a conscious strategy on her part to refocus me and help me cope with the emotional stress I was experiencing. It would be just like her to think up a strategy to bring calm to a stressful situation. She was a true healer.

Sister Perpetua had a way of meeting us where we were, and she always spoke at our level to ensure we understood what she was communicating. This explains why I was both intrigued and baffled by something she shared with our class one morning. She had been away for a few days taking care of her dying sister, and upon her return to class spoke to us at great length about having been with her beloved sibling when she died. She shared with us her experience of how beautiful the moment of her sister's death had been. I remember being very confused and unsettled by her description of the final hours with her sister. How could death possibly be described as beautiful? At that time in my life I understood death as a profoundly sad time, when you lose someone you love. I was totally mystified, therefore, by the thought of someone finding beauty in death!

Sister Perpetua's comments stayed with me for many years, and the concept of a beautiful death continued to elude me. It was almost thirty years later, at age forty-eight, before I would come to understand the meaning of what Sr. Perpetua had shared with our class that day. As I watched my dad die of Alzheimer's, at last being freed from the shadow of a body that could no longer house and carry the fullness of his spirit, I had a glimpse of the beauty Sr. Perpetua had spoken of years earlier, when I was twelve. God had called my father to a place where his essence would no longer be restricted; the beauty in witnessing that freedom did not remove the sadness of losing him, but it was a feeling as authentic and true as the grief that would follow. At times we hear words spoken and have no understanding of their meaning, until we have a personal experience of whatever it is that the words were describing. Standing at my father's deathbed, I finally understood at my core what it was that Sister Perpetua had felt at her sister's deathbed. As an educator this is an important reminder for me to trust in the seeds I plant today, for they may flourish in the minds and hearts of students tomorrow. It is also a reminder to take time with people, because you never know what significance your presence and your words may hold for them.

At my Catholic elementary school, grade seven was the year you were confirmed as an adult in the faith. Part of the confirmation process involved picking the name of a saint that would become your confirmation name. As my fellow classmates clamoured for the saints books to research what name they would pick, I sat still in my desk. I knew exactly the name I would choose. My confirmation name would be Perpetua, the same name my grade seven teacher and mentor had chosen to mark an important transition in her own life. It was the practice at the time, when a woman became a member of a religious community, for her to symbolize her new life with God by choosing a new name. On the evening of my confirmation ceremony Sr. Perpetua quietly pulled me aside and tucked a small gift into my hand, and with a glisten in her eye told me she was glad there was now another Perpetua in the world.

At Christmas time that year, Sr. Perpetua gave each of us a cardboard pop-out of a nativity scene. On the back she had inscribed a single handwritten line, "Please pray for me, as I will for you." For the past number of years I have downsized the Christmas decorations in my home but there will never be a Christmas when I do not set out that precious, now rather tattered and faded nativity card. In the Christian tradition, nativity scenes are a reminder that Jesus is God incarnate, God coming into the world in the fullness of humanity: *Emmanuel, God with us*. How perfect. That is exactly what Sr. Perpetua was for me, God alive and well in a human person.

After I graduated from high school I heard that Sister Perpetua, along with other religious women, had returned to using the name given to her at birth. Sister Perpetua was now Sister Grace. At the time I did not appreciate the appropriateness of her birth name, but I certainly do now. Without doubt this fiery, faith-filled, passionate nun was indeed grace to me. She taught me lessons that are now embedded in my being. She lived life rooted in the belief that God is not far away, and in doing so gave me an experience of a loving God who is reachable. She gave me a glimpse of God at play, and showed me that God celebrates and delights in all of us. She helped me come to see that God is found in laughter and in music, as well as in loss and sadness. And she showed that God could even make death beautiful.

It was many years ago that I received word that Sister Perpetua had died. It is unfortunate that sometimes we do not fully understand the significant role people have played in our lives until much time has passed, and it is too late to offer our personal thanks. I wish I had made an opportunity to thank Sr. Perpetua for being the important *spirit guide* she was for me. She planted and nurtured understandings in me that are still growing and deepening today. She planted a deep desire in me to come to know God and be responsive to God's movement in my life.

Even though I did not have the opportunity to offer my personal thanks to Sr. Perpetua, somehow I know she hears me as I write these words today. My guess is that in place of words, Sr. Perpetua would prefer I thank her by the witness of my life, by striving to be a compassionate *spirit guide* for others, as she was for me. I also highly suspect she is scrunching her nose in my face yet again, and with a twinkle in her eye saying, "I hear you Joan Perpetua, you are most welcome, now get back out on the field and do what you are called to do!"

Later, in my university theological studies, I would come to "meet" the young woman who eventually came to be known in Christian tradition as Saint Perpetua. In reading her engaging life story and tragic end (she was martyred for her faith), I would learn that she was a strong, faith-filled, courageous young woman. How appropriate it would be, therefore, when many centuries later a young nun by the name of Grace Heffernan would take the name Perpetua for her own. As for me, I am extremely proud and deeply humbled to share the name Perpetua with two incredible women who have walked before me, filled with the compassionate and courageous spirit of God.

COMPANION ON THE JOURNEY

Four decades of life have unfolded since my time spent in that grade seven class with Sister Perpetua, and I am incredibly thankful for the foundational beliefs that have remained constant: in particular, the belief in a loving God who is always near. This core belief was to become a stronghold and anchor for me some thirty years later, when I found myself on rocky terrain seriously questioning the early beliefs taught to me by Catholicism. In my early forties I began to experience the Church as limiting. It teachings felt too small to hold the deepening experience of the God I was coming to know within. I underwent a process of unlearning more than learning, as layer by layer I peeled back and examined what I had been taught. It felt disorienting to sense the theological floor I stood upon shifting under me. Very few people around me seemed to find themselves in this same place, so I felt alone and quite displaced. I found myself asking new questions for which old answers no longer sufficed.

During this spiritually turbulent time, I reflected on what had brought me to this "foreign land." As a young girl, and into adulthood, I was deeply involved in the Church. My choice of profession reflected this investment, as I pursued a career as a high school religious education teacher. As I continued to mature, think more critically, and evolve spiritually, however, I began to seriously question a number of Church teachings that I believed were rooted in patriarchy, misogyny, and homophobia. The emotional hurt I saw these teachings cause people unsettled me and conflicted with my belief in a God that is compassionate and inclusive. Simply stated, the God I had come to know and trust was not reflected in what I was experiencing at that time within the Catholic Church. The Church's God felt too small and too limited for me. That God felt judgmental and exclusive, and the loving God I had come to know was inclusive and embraced everyone. I began to see, and experience on a personal level, the Church as more controlling than redeeming. As much as I knew many Catholic leaders to be incredibly good, faith-filled human beings, I no longer wanted to identify myself with a number of the things the institutional Church stood for.

My spiritual life was nudging me onto an undiscovered path, and although it felt unsettling, I knew in the fabric of my being that I needed to trust the movement of the spirit and move into unexplored terrain. I could not run back to the security of the known even if I wanted to, because now it too felt foreign and no longer fit. As unsettling as the unknown felt, I knew it was important that I sit in the discomfort and loneliness of this in-between time, so I struggled hard to surrender and trust that God had led me to this place for a reason. Thankfully, I would not feel alone for very long because God, at the opportune time, sent me another *spirit guide*, this time in the form of an educational colleague, Patti.

Patti, as I would discover, was walking her own unique spiritual path, and unbeknownst to her would become a compass for me as I navigated mine. Adrienne Rich, the notable American poet, states, "The most important thing one woman can do for another is to illuminate and expand her sense of actual possibilities." This statement was never truer than when I worked alongside Patti and learned from her. Patti deeply valued spirituality and was dedicated to the development of the inner life. She became one of my first colleagues and friends, within a Catholic educational context, to intelligently, sensitively, and respectfully critique the Catholic tradition. Patti would be one of the first women I came to work with who did not apologize for naming the reality that for her the Catholic Church did not hold the fullness of how she had come to experience herself, the diverse people around her, her world, and her God. Witnessing the freedom she gave herself to honour her beliefs was profoundly significant for my life's journey. Patti seemed to be in a similar place in her spiritual life. It was incredibly reassuring to know that God had led someone else there, and it was liberating to see Patti not making apologies for it. Seeing my companion Patti on a similar journey, I was more readily able to trust that God had led me there too. In sharing the honesty of her spiritual journey, Patti freed me from the disquiet, guilt, and shame I had been feeling for allowing myself to think, feel, and experience God outside the confines of the Catholic Church. It was not that I felt the Church was innately evil, or intentionally trying to thwart my spiritual growth, I was just finding a number of Church teachings too limiting and too small. The freedom Patti gave herself to explore her spiritual life, in an unencumbered way, served as a profound witness to me. Patti modelled fearless faith, and in doing so freed me to explore the emerging spiritual questions that were agitating my soul in the healthiest of ways.

In courageously working through her own spiritual questions, Patti enabled me to be open and accepting of mine. It was important that it be a woman who modelled inner freedom for me, because for too long I had lived within, and abided by, the secondary role the institutional Church allots to women. The process of asking new questions, as unsettling as it felt at the time, led me to increased spiritual freedom. When I think of the important contribution Patti made to my life, and continues to make, I am reminded of the last line of a beautiful prayer entitled *Inner Freedom* by Joyce Rupp: "Wings, wings, remember your wings!" I will always be indebted to Patti for helping me remember my wings.

Patti retired from education well over a decade ago, but she did not retire from her commitment to inner growth. She spent a number of years studying to become a Jungian analyst. Her desire to be an analyst flowed out of the work she had been doing with her own analyst for many years. Throughout Patti's studies we had occasion to get together, and when we would meet I would find myself totally captivated by the richness of her experience. I felt inspired by the many insights she shared, and over time I felt called to begin Jungian analysis myself. I would have loved for Patti to be my analyst, but professional ethics disallowed it, given our friendship. I looked to Patti to suggest a person with whom I might do this important work. Patti suggested one of her supervisors, Graham, as possibly being a good fit for me. Little did I know that in connecting me with Graham, Patti was leading me right to the doorstep of my next *spirit guide.*

GROWING IN CONSCIOUSNESS

As I entered Jungian analysis I knew I would need to trust in the process and be committed for an extended period of time. Although I was excited to begin analysis, I felt a level of anxiety, which for me always accompanies the unknown. My first session with Graham was set for the end of November, which is the time of year the Christian tradition marks as the beginning of Advent. As I drove to my first session, I was struck by the appropriateness of the timing: Advent is a season of anticipation and hope. It was in that spirit that I made my way to Graham's home that evening.

My heart and soul were ripe for deepening, but I was a bit tentative about where my analysis sessions would lead. I was then reminded of a story Patti had shared about a woman, who in the process of inquiring about doing analysis with her, said, "I want to do this work but not if it is going to ask me to make major changes in my life!" Patti's honest response was to encourage the woman to come to analysis with an open mind and heart: the work involved bringing the self to deeper integration, and at the beginning one could not predict what might be asked of the self, to move in that direction. In light of Patti's wise advice, I tried to position myself in a place of openness and trust. I knew the richness of the learning and the depth of growth would be in proportion to how honest I was willing to be with self. I suspected that courage would be needed, because analysis would involve looking at the shadow (the parts of ourselves we do not want to look at or own), and other complexes, to help render conscious what is unconscious. I began preparing myself for the fact that the work would undoubtedly be uncomfortable and challenging at times, but I trusted that the hard work would be worth the investment, since it would lead me to fuller integration of self and hopefully to greater personal freedom.

As I entered the back door of Graham's tranquil home in Toronto, I felt an openness of mind and heart and was ready to begin a new and important chapter in my spiritual journey. My connection with Graham was immediate. His humble approach, gentle manner, and well-developed sense of humour endeared me to him. I felt reassured that I was sitting across from a man I could trust. My first session went well, and upon arriving home I wrote in my journal: *I am amazed at how one hour with a stranger quickly became the birthplace of an emerging self. I sense that my sessions with Graham will be a hearth for the sparks that will enflame my soul.* The initial insight I recorded that evening has proven true. Working with Graham has indeed fanned the sparks of a deepening self, and has contributed in significant ways to the enlargement of my soul. Jungian analysis has become profound and sacred work for me. As my analyst, Graham has become a significant *spirit guide* by directing me in gentle yet pointed ways on the path of self-discovery. Graham's expertise, sensitivity, and intuition have been guiding lights in directing my exploration of self, and I have gained sometimes subtle, sometimes profound, but always wise insights along the way.

The most important insights I have gained have evolved from a fundamental challenge Graham placed before me at the outset of our work together. He encouraged me to develop a new relationship with self. He pointed out that as an extrovert, I am quite confident and comfortable processing things on the outside, but he challenged me to turn my attention to the inside, to my interior life. I accepted his challenge, and the movement from outside to inside has proven to be an important and significant shift for me.

Dream analysis has facilitated access to my unconscious and helped me concentrate on my interior life. As I shared my initial dreams with Graham in my early sessions he noted how many of my dreams were filled, if not overwrought, with people busying themselves in different directions. He humbly suggested that my unconscious was acknowledging that I was a person well versed in *doing,* and was now calling me to more *being*. Over time I would come to see that the challenge to *being,* and to nurturing a rich interior life, was at the heart of all of the work I would do with Graham. Nurturing an interior life would end up facilitating a life more consciously lived, and would become a conduit for growing my soul.

Although paying attention to one's interior life is a rich experience, it can be incredibly challenging, because it demands taking an honest look at self. What I quickly came to realize was how often in life I had put others under a magnifying glass rather than taking a good look in the mirror! I began to acknowledge how often I had blamed conflict on the inadequacies of other people: "If only other people had seen the error of *their* ways, things would have gone much more smoothly!" Once I started letting go of the belief that broken and strained relationships were about the faults and foibles of others, I began to take ownership for my contribution to the breakdown of these relationships. One of the most significant insights I have gained from working with Graham is that much of what I thought was about others is really about me. If you do not think this is a humbling place to find yourself, think again! Graham has assisted me in becoming more personally accountable, and in doing so has helped me take increased responsibility for my life.

Part of Jungian analysis involves looking at one's shadow, and other complexes, all of which emerge at some point in your dreams. Working with the shadow demands taking an honest look at the things about yourself that you find undesirable, and therefore have chosen to avoid. It means owning parts of yourself you would rather not acknowledge, let alone embrace. Part of the process is being asked to lower the protective shield you have been hiding behind in order to peel back layer upon layer of feelings, whatever they may be. These feelings often include shame, guilt, fear, insecurity, and inadequacy. Shadow work is difficult work and can leave one feeling emotionally and spiritually naked. It is understandable, therefore, why many people run from the work of the soul. Standing in a place of vulnerability is unsettling and uncomfortable to most people. Looking at one's shadow is humbling because it involves digging deep and getting painfully real with self.

Graham has been an important *spirit guide* in helping me see, acknowledge, and "unpack" my shadow. The trust relationship I share with him has given me the courage and confidence to let down some of my defences in order to do this work. With expertise and gentleness, Graham has helped me explore my shadow (among other complexes), and has led me to a deeper awareness of self, helping me become more conscious. Since working with him, I am more able to see and name for myself that which keeps me from being freer, emotionally and spiritually.

As well as exploring my shadow, another key area of focus in my sessions with Graham has been the role of feminine (anima) and masculine (animus) energy. Carl Jung suggests that women and men have masculine and feminine energy, and that both energies need healthy expression in the inner and outer worlds. Masculine energy is that energy that prompts us to "go for it." It is reflected in Nike's motto, "Just do it!" Masculine energy is *doing* energy. Feminine energy is relational energy, and is receptive and intuitive. It is *being* energy.

Graham and I have shared many soulful dialogues about the role masculine and feminine energies have played in my life. He has helped me understand that it is masculine energy that has given me the confidence and assurance to function well in the *outside* world. For example, it has been animus (masculine) *doing* energy that has propelled me forward, enabling me to attain many personal and professional goals. I have come to understand that I use masculine energy in my outer world with ease and confidence. Another thing Graham has helped me identify, however, is that I have failed to use this same energy in my *inner* world, where it is needed to maintain balance. The absence of masculine energy in my inner world has been problematic, because it has created imbalance in my relationships with others, and with self. I will try to elucidate here by sharing a bit about my personal and professional relationships.

In past relationships (both personal and professional) I have found it difficult to assert my own needs. In my personal life, my pattern has been to acquiesce to the needs of a partner rather than ensure my needs are given equal consideration. This has frequently resulted in feelings of resentment on my part, because I did not believe partners were meeting my needs or taking responsibility for their own needs. But who really had the problem? It is my responsibility to name my needs and share them with my partner. In times where I felt my partner's needs were overshadowing my own, it was *my* responsibility to speak up. Instead, I would grow silent and resentful, expecting my partner to be a mind reader and know what my needs were. Through analysis, I have come to understand that I would enjoy healthier relationships if I used animus (masculine) energy in my inner world to establish healthy boundaries, and ensure my needs are not swallowed up in the process of trying to meet the needs of others. I have been working at establishing healthy boundaries in my relationships for the past number of years, and am finding that it goes a long way in reducing the amount of resentment I feel toward people. Establishing healthy boundaries also helps me honour myself more fully by being attentive and responsive to my own needs.

I have come to understand the benefits of using masculine energy in my personal life, but also in my professional life. For many years I found it difficult to say "no" when asked to do certain work at school. I felt a degree of ego satisfaction being called upon by colleagues or supervisors to perform work tasks or be part of committees. I acknowledge that sharing one's talents and skills is inherently good, but through Graham's insights I have come to see that when I found myself always saying "yes," something was operating on an unconscious level, and I was overextending and exhausting myself in the process! He has helped me understand that saying "yes" can evolve from a desire to please others and has suggested that when we are "pleasers," difficult questions are begging to be asked, most notably, is my self-worth inextricably tied into my professional performance. Is my work *persona* my core identity? Do I have a deep-seated need to be needed, and is this central to my feelings of self-worth? Graham has wisely cautioned me to live *in* my job but not *be* of it. I think this is very wise advice. I have observed a number of people experiencing great difficulty when retiring. Why is this so? I think in some cases it may be because their core identity is intricately tied into their work persona. Retirement forces us to face the difficult question of who we are outside of our work.

I am glad that I have evolved in consciousness in this area, because now I am more apt to use masculine energy in my inner world to draw lines in the sand and say "no" when needed. This has created better balance in my outer world. I have come to understand that part of the reason I frequently said "yes" in the past was due to my ego's need for strokes, which had evolved from feelings of inadequacy. On some level I felt I needed to earn my worth. Graham and I have talked about how this may relate to my being gay. It is not uncommon for gay people to feel they have to earn people's love and respect. Overall, it has been very liberating to explore why I was a "yes" woman for so long. I like to think that I have evolved to at least a "let me think more about it" woman!

Not long ago I was lying on my couch at home feeling exhausted after a hectic work week. Every day that week, I had been trying to solve people's problems and ensure the tasks I performed were well done. As I lay on the couch I ruminated on how I had brought this feeling of fatigue on myself. I knew I had only myself to blame for my exhaustion, and realized, yet again, how tiring and unpleasant martyrdom felt! I smiled to myself, because in that conscious moment of taking responsibility for self, I saw that there might be hope for me yet!

Another important area Graham has helped me explore is my emotional life. He has helped me develop a healthy relationship with emotions I had detached from, predominantly anger and sadness. From my studies in psychology, I am aware that feelings do not go away without being acknowledged. They are like impatient visitors on a doorstep, knocking and wanting to come in, and if their knock goes unheeded they knock louder, for, as Carl Jung said, what we resist persists. My sessions with Graham have assisted me in letting the unwelcome guests in so I might come to understand them and be taught by them.

I think one of the reasons I have struggled with the open expression of emotion is the result of early messages I received about them, particularly about the expression of sadness. When I was sixteen, my cousin Paul died of muscular dystrophy. He was only seventeen years of age. Paul's family and my family grew up together, so Paul was like a brother to me. He was a big part of my life, and my entire family's life. After his death people rarely spoke about him, at least not around me. I do not point this out to allot blame, for I acknowledge that people grieve in their own ways and this needs to be respected. I share this observation simply to explain why the expression of sadness may have become an issue for me as an adult. In the experience of the profound loss of Paul, I learned that pain can hurt so much, and run so deep, that people just want to forget, and I internalized the message that pushing feelings down is the way to cope with heartache.

As I grew into adulthood I knew intellectually that expressing feelings was healthy, both on an emotional and physical level, but my cognitive knowledge did not express itself in action. I often held back emotion, even at funerals, where tears were expected and socially acceptable. I feared that crying would be seen as a sign of weakness, and render me vulnerable. I used humour as a way to avoid expressing sadness and anger, and over time it became a dependable crutch to lean on in order to cover up my real emotions. Unfortunately, using humour to divert is an avoidance strategy that comes with strong external validation. After all, who doesn't like a person who is funny and makes them laugh? But the joking on the outside was a cover-up for feelings on the inside. Not being able to openly express my emotions led to dissonance, and over time I wanted to be more congruent and authentic.

My sessions with Graham allowed me to grow in conscious awareness by understanding that I do not need walls to protect myself from my feelings. My work with him has enabled me to trust myself more fully so I can let down my guard and express emotion. I have evolved to a place where I know that my world will not crumble if I express sadness or anger, and I have come to realize that the people who love me will not love me less if I express on the outside what I feel on the inside.

I have come to see that the more I befriend my emotions the more comfortable I am with other people's expression of emotion. This is far from coincidence, because until people are able to embrace their own emotions they will not be comfortable seeing emotion expressed by others. This is due to their own level of discomfort with these same emotions. This is called a projection. A number of years back I found myself caught in a friend's projection. I was attending the funeral service of the mother of a very dear friend, and due to a severe snowstorm the night before, I was unable to attend the visitation. The first time I was able to see my friend since hearing of her mother's death was at the end of the service, when she was walking in procession behind the coffin. As my friend exited the church she looked my way, and I was grabbed with emotion and began to cry. At around the same time another friend was walking down the aisle, and when she saw me crying she grabbed me by the arm, and in a teasing voice said to me, "What are *you* crying about?" I did not respond verbally. I just smiled through my tears and let them continue to flow. If this same situation had occurred earlier in my life, I would have felt embarrassed by my tears and quickly regrouped by drying them. Now, not only was I allowing myself to feel what I was feeling, but was giving myself permission to openly express my emotions. It felt good to express on the outside the feelings I had on the inside. In reflecting on this experience, I am led to wonder if the friend who grabbed my arm is trapped in the same emotional place I was for many years.

Through analysis I have come to understand that my years of personal discomfort with the open expression of emotion were reflective of my inability to be "at home" with my own emotions, to embrace them from within. Given my years of practice with keeping sadness and anger at bay, I know it will take ongoing effort for me to let them "through the door." I will need to consciously combat the messages I have received over the years, both implicitly and explicitly, from my family of origin and from the world around me, messages that have encouraged me to keep emotions at a "respectable" distance. But hope lies in the awareness I have now that I did not have before, of the damage those internalized messages did to self.

By sharing a brief exchange I had with one of my students, I will highlight one of the other key areas Graham has led me to explore. Our high school has a policy that disallows students from wearing hats inside the building. As long as there are rules, there will be teenagers trying to push the limits of these rules, so there is a young man who day after day continues to challenge school policy by wearing a ball cap. OBEY is the inscription on the top of his hat, and the irony never escapes me when I frequently have to ask him to obey the school rules by removing it from his head! There is a whole line of OBEY clothing products worn by teenagers, and each time I read the word etched on a hat or a hoodie I am reminded of a challenge Graham presented to me. He suggested that at times we must be willing to disobey because it is healthy to do so. Graham has explained that in freeing ourselves from rules and set ways of doing things, we allow ourselves to be creative and spontaneous, and will see things we may currently be blind to. Graham is referring to the need at times to challenge the *collective*.

Although the *collective* works in positive ways, by ensuring certain norms are adhered to in the interests of all, sometimes the *collective* works in negative ways by making people feel like they have to act in accordance with certain *shoulds*. Some examples include: All married people *should* have children. All women *should* stay home with their children until their children are school age. All men *should* hide their emotions. These are but a few examples of how *collective* thinking can keep people locked into set ways of thinking and acting, based on the belief that this is how things *must* be done. I would guess that most of us could identify a situation where we have been shored up against a *should* and have fallen short! "Should-itis" leaves little room for individual freedom. It discourages creative expression, and ultimately dampens the soul.

Some people become so absorbed in the *collective* that they do not question it, or even believe it needs questioning. These people blindly accept *shoulds* as the way things are intended to be, and struggle with people who "rock the boat." A good question to ask a person who is entrenched in *collective* thinking, and therefore tells you what you *should* do, is to ask them respectfully "Says who?" Most likely this will stop them in their tracks because they have never dared to question the *shoulds*. They may have no response to offer beyond, "That is just the way it *should* be!" or "That is the way it has always been!"

Graham has pointed out that marginalized groups in society live on the fringe, outside the *collective*, and from this vantage point are able to constructively critique it. He has suggested that certain freedoms come from living on the margins and not being fully immersed in the *collective*. Graham has identified gay people as one group that lives on the margins. As a gay woman I can certainly think of examples of where living on the margins has brought me personal freedom. One example has to do with freedom from set sex roles. When in relationship with another woman, I never feel pressure to perform tasks based on my gender. When involved in gay partnerships, my partner and I have never assumed set roles. We have performed whatever tasks and roles have best suited our interests and abilities. In heterosexual relationships, however, I observe roles being more set and established, most often based on gender. Studies indicate, for example, that women in heterosexual partnerships still complete the vast majority of housekeeping and childcare tasks. A number of my heterosexual female friends are hard on themselves, feeling they *should* be able to be supermom and superwife, and do it all!

Even though I am a member of a group that lives on the margins, I still feel pressured at times to abide by *shoulds*, but dialoguing with Graham has brought me increased freedom and led me to challenge them. I am more conscious of the role I allow the *collective* to play in my decision-making, and have chosen to be more honest with myself by taking the time to stop and discern whether I really want to do something I am thinking about doing. At times I have allowed myself to be sucked in by the *collective* and done things out of a sense of obligation — succumbing to the pressure of what I felt I *should* do. Sometimes I have folded under the pressure and repressed what I wanted to do in order to avoid hurting someone, or a group of people. Putting the *collective* into proper perspective has been incredibly liberating. It has felt as if I have discovered for the first time that there is a doorknob on both sides of a door, and instead of waiting for the *collective* to open the door for me, I have opened it for myself. I have come to learn that sometimes we have to exercise our personal power by opening the door ourselves and walking through. I have come to understand that it is perfectly acceptable to make choices that are in line with one's personal integrity and vision for how one wants to live one's life, even if it means "rocking the boat." I am no longer as willing to give in to the voice of the *collective*, which tells me to wait dutifully until it deems when and if the door should be opened.

There is a lot of pressure to buy into the *collective*, therefore we need to proceed consciously and avoid being drawn into its vortex, where we risk losing ourselves in the process. The *collective* is pervasive, and functions within institutions as well as within individuals. As mentioned in chapter two, it was less than easy getting explicit supports in place for sexual-minority students in a Catholic school, due to the collective pressure to avoid sensitive and highly politicized issues. It is far easier to go with the flow, and give in to the *collective* because people who dare to challenge it encounter pushback. "Obey and all shall be well" seems to be the sentiment. There are times, however, when we need to face the wind head on, and challenge the status quo. Human beings are not meant to be force-fitted into moulds, or move forward in one set formation. That is predictability, not living.

I think many people adhere to the collective because it provides them with a feeling of security and a sense of belonging. One might ask, what is wrong with that? The problem lies in the reality that while providing some people with a sense of security, the *collective* leaves other people feeling excluded. I think of the highly creative individuals in our world. They frequently get criticized and judged because their feet always stick outside the conventional box. Individual expression and diversity can be sacrificed on the altar of commonality and uniformity. Perhaps this is why I have always appreciated the rebels in the world, who call us to new ways of seeing, believing, and being. When my mother sees someone acting outside the norm of how people commonly act, she turns and says to me, "Different strokes for different folks!" Wouldn't it be wonderful if individuals and institutions openly celebrated the "different strokes by different folks" and welcomed all? When thinking about inspiring people who bravely challenged the collective, I think of Jesus. His words and actions frequently challenged the status quo as he compassionately reached out to include and affirm those who lived on the margins.

It is difficult to be a person who challenges the collective. It led Jesus to the cross. People not adhering to the *collective* are forced to swim upstream; only the courageous dare to swim against the stream. Many of them become tired of the constant battle, and turn around and swim in formation with all the others. There is, after all, far more societal reward in going along with the crowd, doing what is expected, than for carving a unique path. I think the next time I see that student wearing the OBEY hat, instead of asking him to remove it, I will take a marker and write DIS in front of OBEY and walk away …that should be good for a parent call or two!

SYMBOLIC NIGHT VISITORS

As I mentioned previously, dream analysis is a significant part of the work I do in my sessions with Graham. Interpreting the symbols of one's dreams helps bring that which is unconscious to consciousness, and in this way deepen one's understanding of self, eventually moving one to a place of fuller integration. The unconscious always desires that we be whole. Looking at the reoccurring patterns in our dreams is one way to discern the unconscious' attempt to move us to greater wholeness. One of the patterns that have emerged in my dreams is the presence of young males. Graham has helped me unpack the meaning of these symbolic night visitors through a Jungian lens, by explaining that young male figures represent masculine energy that is spontaneous, creative, curious, and playful. Therefore, the ongoing appearance of young masculine images in my dreams is my unconscious calling me to healthier balance in my life.

The responsibilities that come with being a high school administrator are vast, and can frequently leave one feeling exhausted. It is important, therefore, for me to be attentive to the young masculine images at night that call me to a lighter way of being. Their invitation to be creative and spontaneous is an important reminder for me to put down the "tools of my trade" and go out and play. How unwise it would be for me to turn my back on them! In no way have I achieved total balance in my life, so I am grateful for these wise imps who grace my dreams, tap me on the shoulder, and beckon me to join them for the sake of health and wellness.

This coming fall I will be moving into my eighth year in Jungian analysis. My hour with Graham has become my *appointment with self*, my time to stop and understand what has been, so that I may move into what is yet to come more consciously. Each session with him has helped me put another puzzle piece on the table, and over time I am seeing the evolving picture that is me. I know that trying to live more consciously will be a lifelong life quest, and I am deeply committed to the process, because it has been liberating to face and understand a number of issues that held me hostage.

The underlying goal of Jungian analysis is individuation, moving to fuller integration and wholeness. My commitment to the work is grounded in my belief that the further I move toward individuation (wholeness), the freer I will live, and the clearer glimpse I will have of the divine within. As I grow in consciousness and become deepened as an individual, it is my hope that I will become a more compassionate presence, and will help expand the consciousness of the world.

As a *spirit guide*, Graham, like Sister Perpetua and Patti, has been an invaluable gift to my life. I believe that God sent these *spirit guides* my way at the precise time needed to direct me on my spiritual path. Each of them in their own humble and wise way has led me to deeper understandings, and has opened doors that have enabled me to love myself, and others, more freely. For this, and for all the wisdom my *spirit guides* have led me to, I am profoundly grateful.

As I continue my life's journey I trust that other *spirit guides* will cross my path and walk beside me. Like Sister Perpetua, Patti, and Graham, they will teach me lessons needed for further deepening, and the insights and wisdom they offer will enrich the next chapters of my life. Looking ahead to the many different experiences I am yet to encounter, I feel gratitude for what will remain constant throughout, which is the assurance that no matter where life leads me I will always be *guided by grace*.

My greatest teachers are the people who have helped me come to wisdom, rather than give it to me.

Deepening Your Life...

Who have been the spirit guides in your life? What wisdom have they led you to?

Has your image and experience of God changed from when you were young? If so, how? Has this change made a difference in how you relate to God, self, and others?

Have you ever come to a place where your old answers no longer satisfied new questions? How did this place feel for you? What new questions have you been led to ask? What insight(s) have you gained from asking these questions?

What "unlearning" have you done in your life? What new learning was found in the "unlearning"?

What are you more conscious of about yourself today than you were a decade ago? Has this deepened self-awareness enriched your life and relationships with self, God and others? If so, in what way(s)?

Identify some of the "shoulds" in your life. How are they keeping you from being free? What might you be called to do outside of the collective that would ultimately bring you increased freedom and fulfillment?

Which energy, (feminine) being or (masculine) doing, do you use most in your inner world? In your outer world? What energy do you need to use more frequently to achieve greater balance and wholeness?

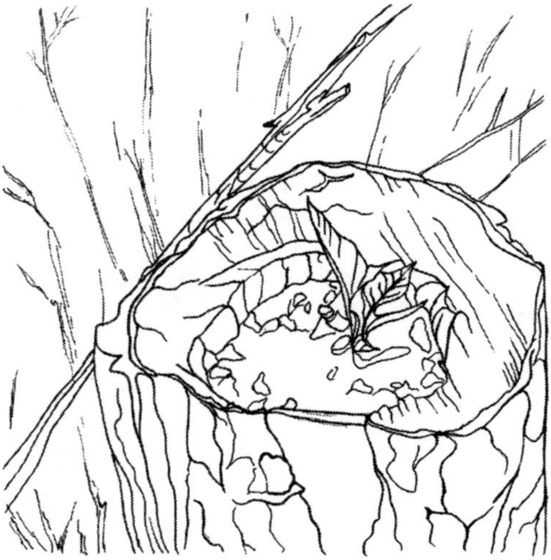

CHAPTER FOUR

Loving, Learning, and Letting Go

THE SELF IN RELATIONSHIP

Over the years, an area of focus and study that has held deep interest for me is relationships. In my own experience, relationships have been both a gift and a struggle. They have been the reason my heart has overflowed, feeling full and alive, and the reason it has felt torn apart and at times inconsolable. Regardless of the circumstances, all my relationships have been open doors inviting me to learn more about self and others.

For a number of years I taught a high school leadership course that included a unit on relationships. I know if I were to teach that unit today, my starting point would be quite different. Instead of moving directly to an analysis of healthy and unhealthy relationships, I would begin with an intensive focus on the *individual* in relationship because the quality of the relationships we share is, first and foremost, a reflection of how we feel about ourselves and how we teach others to treat us.

I have come to see over time, and quite honestly through much struggle, that it is vital to develop a healthy relationship with self before partnering with another. It is important to strive to become a whole person within so that one does not feel incomplete and compelled to be out in the world desperately searching for one's "better half." The movie Jerry Maguire comes to mind with its infamous line, "You complete me." That sentiment may make for great movies, but in the world of real relationships it is a recipe for disaster, because its underlying assumption is that we need another person to make us feel whole inside. It is not fair or healthy to expect another human being to ensure *we* feel complete. It is our own responsibility to work toward feeling whole as a person, and not the job of someone else to do this *for* us.

Asking people to take responsibility for themselves in relationship does not mean it is unacceptable or unhealthy to place reasonable expectations on the person we share a relationship with. It is reasonable, for example, to expect our partner to be committed to us. It is fair to expect that they will contribute to the enhancement of our life and strive to love us unconditionally. It is not fair, however, to expect them to complete us. Entering a relationship with the expectation that the other person will complete us is fertile ground for breeding dependent and co-dependent relationships. These types of relationships are unhealthy and do not foster mutual growth in individuals or in partnerships. Dependent and co-dependent relationships keep people stuck in repetitive holding patterns that disallow movement in any positive direction.

I have spent time with couples who are stuck in unhealthy relationships. It is a sad situation on a number of levels, not the least of which is the resentment and hostility frequently present, which often gets expressed in passive-aggressive ways. It is difficult to watch people tear each other down instead of build each other up. Some couples know their relationships are not healthy or bringing happiness, but feel paralyzed to do anything about it. This leads one to wonder why people choose to stay in lifeless relationships for so long. The answer lies in acknowledging how powerful, debilitating, and paralyzing fear can be. Fear has a way of sinking its roots deep down, and it manifests itself in many different ways. Some people have a deep-seated fear of being alone, and therefore feel that even a stagnant, unhealthy relationship is better than no relationship at all. Other people fear hurting their partner if they try to change or leave the relationship, even if the cost of staying in the relationship is damaging to self, and ultimately to their partner as well. Some individuals fear disappointing the people and institutions closest to them (their family or church, for example), and worry about losing their love and support if they do not uphold the expectations placed upon them to stay in their present situation. Some individuals fear the financial loss that may accompany the termination of a relationship. Some people fear being loved unconditionally, due to never having been loved in this way before — unconditional love feels foreign to them and leaves them feeling scared and incredibly vulnerable. Instead of working through the fear, in order to open themselves up to being loved in a healthy way, they choose to stay in what they perceive as the security and safety of a known relationship, even if the relationship is unhealthy and joyless. No matter how fear shows itself, it is often an emotion that overwhelms people and keeps them immobilized and "living" in unhealthy holding patterns for a very long time. I qualify the word "living" because couples finding themselves in unhealthy relationships are often not truly living at all, but merely surviving.

It takes courage and strength, and deep faith in oneself, to face fear head on. Many people do not feel up to the challenge, and opt to stay in unhealthy relationships for years, some for a lifetime. Some couples sit idly, hoping something will happen externally to magically turn things around. They cling to the erroneous belief that some outside influence will eventually come along and unstick them, only to discover that nothing changes and no one is coming to save them.

There are some courageous individuals who eventually move out of unhealthy relationships. By doing the inner work necessary and taking responsibility for themselves, they are able to move to a much healthier place. Looking back, they see how trapped they kept themselves, and feel good in their heart knowing that they have now made the right decision. Over time they come to see that they not only set themselves free, but their partner as well. It takes tremendous strength and courage to break out of an unhealthy relationship, so perhaps it should not be surprising that many people stay right where they are, turning their backs on the inner stirrings of their soul that are beckoning them to a healthier way of being. It is an unfortunate reality that some people live their entire lives within the confines of an unhealthy relationship because, at a conscious or unconscious level, they believe they are not deserving or worthy of being loved unconditionally.

Having had the experience of being involved in an unhealthy relationship, I can identify and empathize with people caught in such partnerships. In my particular situation, I made the choice to wait in the wings for someone I deeply loved to take steps to be free to explore a relationship with me. After a number of years this never came to fruition. I do not place blame on the other person. I could have left the unhealthy situation at any time. It was I who made the choice to trust in what I was being told and wait for a number of years. During this time I struggled to muster the emotional fortitude to walk away once and for all, and let go of the "us" that I felt was never given a chance. Having had this experience, I appreciate how stuck one can feel, and how hard it is to find the strength to walk away. For me the strength to leave came from the realization that I was not showing myself any respect in choosing to remain. I finally came to see that the relationship was a dead end, and that it was slowly moving me away from who I understood myself to be. Over time I grew tired of feeling the pain and hurt that came from living a life dissonant with my integrity and core spirit. I am thankful for the positive self-esteem I possessed that ultimately enabled me to move out of the situation and treat myself more kindly and more respectfully.

It took a number of years, but eventually I came to the place where I was no longer willing to feed that which was damaging to my soul. I smile at the irony of the fact that I told the other person — who had assured me time and time again that her present relationship was over — "If the horse is dead, get off!" All along I was the one that needed to get off the horse! Talk about the ultimate projection. Obviously I needed to take a good look in the mirror and ask some tough questions: above all, why had I stayed in this unhealthy situation for so long, and why had I allowed myself to be "okay" with getting so little when I had given so much? I knew I needed to figure this out in the interests of my emotional health, and the health of future relationships. Clearly I had work to do in this area, and I consciously set about doing it.

I learned many important lessons from the experience of choosing to stay in an unhealthy relationship. I learned that people who have a pattern of failing to take responsibility for self are not bad people, but they do not make for healthy relationship partners. I learned that we hurt others out of our own woundedness, even if unintentionally. Ultimately, I would learn that many gifts had come from the painful experience. For example, from the depth of feeling angry, alone, and sad arose the gift of humility, as I was forced to look at my role in the unhealthy relationship and admit I had much to learn. I also learned that it was important to go gently and forgive myself, especially at those times when I chastised myself by asking, How could I have chosen to be involved in such an unhealthy situation? How could I have not known better? How could I have not seen things with more clarity at the outset, and in this way avoided all the heartache? I had to remind myself that it can be hard to see people and situations with clarity, since at an unconscious level we often see what we want or *need* to see. This experience reminded me of the importance of conscious self-reflection, which helps us understand why we do what we do. It made me appreciate the importance of growing in self-awareness, which allows us to become more integrated as individuals, and makes us less apt to project our needs onto others. The more integrated we are, the more likely we are to attract individuals who will be a healthy fit for us. Simply stated, we will enjoy healthier relationships, both with self and others, if first and foremost we take responsibility for ourselves and do the emotional work needed.

This raises the question: How does one take responsibility for self? Part of taking responsibility for self involves asking some key questions at the outset of feeling a strong attraction to another person, because often these attractions indicate more about us than they do about the person we are attracted to. I have come to this understanding the hard way. In the past I believed that being infatuated and "crushing out" on someone — feelings most often driven by physical attraction — must be an indicator that the other person is a good match. What I have come to understand is that this can be far from the truth, since such attractions are often more indicative of unfinished business from one's past, pointing to inner work needing to be done, than they are of compatibility with the person we are attracted to. Put another way, developing a crush on someone is often a sign that the other person carries something for us, something that is either underdeveloped or completely undeveloped in us. This may be at the core of the attraction. In these situations we may not be seeing the other person for who they truly are because we are too busy seeing them for who we need them to be *for us*. This is why it makes sense when people talk about feeling an instant attraction to another person, and make statements like, "It is as if I knew them my entire life!" In a very real way they *have* known the other person their whole life, because they are seeing themselves mirrored in that other person! The other person is often reflecting the undeveloped or underdeveloped part of themselves and this explains the strong resonance within. The person we are attracted to has something we want and need, and this is often at the core of the attraction. People will describe the feeling as like a magnet pulling them toward the other. They believe that partnering with the other person will complete them as an individual and make them feel whole, but it will not, because feelings of health and wholeness do not come from the outside in; they come from the inside out.

It is time well spent to reflect on what is truly at work in our instant attraction situations. A healthy approach is to discern what is at the core of our attraction, and set about expressing within ourselves the aspects we are attracted to in the other person. In other words, we must identify what the other person holds for us and develop this quality within, rather than become fused with the other person. In this way, and only in this way, will we ever be free to see the other person for who they truly are, see the person who *is* versus the person we have created. We will also feel more integrated as a person due to the development and expansion of self that occurs in the process. A journal entry I wrote when working through a strong attraction to another person captures the connection between our attraction to others and the inherent invitation to further develop ourselves: *Have I met you before? Are you the part of me longing to be free? This instant connection cannot be far from who I am...an ancient soul finding its way home.*

The degree to which we can allow and free others to be who they truly are is a measurement of the emotional work we have done within. If we are actively doing the work needed to become whole, we will not need people to be anyone or anything other than who they really are. We will have no desire to project our needs onto others, because we will have asked the questions needing to be asked at the level of self. We will have developed what needed to be developed within, so we no longer need to look to others to give it to us. As you can see, there is tremendous potential for us to discover ourselves in relationships!

Projecting our unconscious needs onto others is but one way we create relationships that are unhealthy. Another way we create unhealthy relationships is in attempting to rescue others. This is not healthy for the rescuer or for the person being rescued. I have some experience in this area as well. I did not realize I was a rescuer until into my forties when I began working with a family systems therapist, Gloria, to address issues related to accepting and integrating my same-sex orientation. I was also seeking support to terminate a near decade-long relationship. Gloria guided me with wisdom and sensitivity, and always took an honest "shoot from the hip" approach, which I deeply appreciated. In one session Gloria referred to me as a *potential junkie*. It was her observation that I get so caught up in seeing people's potential that I neglect to see the reality of who the person actually is. She encouraged me to give equal consideration to potential and reality. Gloria drew the parallel between my actions and a mother bird. In order to keep her young happy and content, a mother bird busies herself bringing worms back and forth to the nest. In the same way, I had been busying myself trying to "feed" partners by attempting to rescue them. I consistently took it upon myself to try to help others fulfill the potential I saw in them, and expended a great deal of energy in doing so. At the time I did not identify this behaviour as unhealthy. I felt my intentions were sincere, since I was trying to help the person I cared about. Today I see the error in my thinking. It is admirable to want to support one's partner in the attainment of goals and aspirations, but in attempting to rescue them we are saying we know better than they what is best for them. I now see the fundamental arrogance in this thinking. I also understand that it is not my job to rescue others. As discussed earlier in this chapter, people need to take responsibility for themselves in relationships.

Part of my motivation for rescuing people was to try to help the people I loved avoid pitfalls, and to assist them in digging their way out of challenging predicaments. Rescuing was my attempt to help make the path ahead easier for them. It is here that I recall the wise words of a mentor who once said to me, "Don't deny people their pain: that is how they learn and grow!" How true. Like a caterpillar that must have its time of darkness and struggle in its cocoon — so that one day it can have the inner fortitude and strength to break out, transform into a butterfly, and fly free — so too must we allow this place and space for one another. It is important to stand back and respectfully give others the freedom to face the life lessons and struggles that are theirs to work through. This means resisting the urge to rescue, and instead holding loved ones with open hands and hearts as they navigate their way forward. The hardest part of doing this is to avoid judging or becoming attached to the outcome, and letting people face the consequences of their decisions, whatever they may be. I do not have children of my own, but my sisters and friends who are parents have shared with me that it is extremely difficult to remain detached from the outcome when it comes to their own offspring!

As well as being unhealthy for others, rescuing is emotionally draining and unhealthy for us. In the process of "feeding" others the self starves, which often leads to resentment. As feelings of resentment build, they become toxic to self and to relationships. It serves a person well, therefore, to ask: What is behind my need to rescue people? I am sure there are many possible answers to that question, but I believe that our attempts to rescue others emanate, to some degree, from our need to be needed. Perhaps, due to feelings of inadequacy, we rescue other people in an attempt to feel better about ourselves. We think that having people dependent on us will make us feel needed and loved. In the long haul (and I choose the word *haul* here for good reason), rescuing does not contribute to feelings of being loved. It leaves us feeling emotionally depleted.

Rescuing can also be a subtle passive-aggressive attempt to control people. We need to be wise and discern what we can and cannot control, and what we should and should not try to control. For example, choosing to control our temper or choosing to be kind when we would rather take out our frustration on someone is a good way of exercising control. This has to do with self-control. The problem occurs when we try to control others, because this does not allow them their freedom. Ultimately, trying to control people is wasted energy, because the more we try to exert control over others, the more they tend to resist.

For a number of years I have kept the same poster on my office door at work. It reads, "Those who love us let us find our own way." It is an important reminder to let people "be" and resist the tendency to rescue or control them. In this simple message lies the challenge to let go and trust that people will end up where they are meant to be. The poster cautions against telling other people who they should be and what decisions they should make for their lives. Of course, when invited, it is fully appropriate for us to help people explore their desires and dreams for self, but I have learned that people have their own life lessons to learn, and in *their* own time. It is a lesson in humility to come to that place where you realize that the best way to truly support a loved one is to get out of their way and let them make their own choices and learn their own lessons, even knowing that many of these lessons will be born of heartache and pain.

PAIN AND STRUGGLE AS WISE TEACHERS

As I stated earlier, it is often our unconscious needs that direct how we function in relationships. I know in some of my past relationships I have attracted people who are incredibly good souls but who are not a healthy fit for me. It has been important for my personal growth to ask myself why this has been so. Why do I find myself moving in to rescue others only to find myself totally depleted over time? This pattern is unhealthy in many ways. We only have so much emotional energy in our "well," and our bucket quickly empties in our resolve to fill others up, leaving little or no energy to take care of self. Rescue relationships become recipes for disappointment because somewhere deep down, rescuers hold the expectation that at some point the tables will turn and the person they are rescuing will reciprocate and fill them up. Yet this never happens, because people who are emotionally unavailable to self cannot possibly be emotionally available to others. Meeting the needs of another person without having your own needs met is detrimental to self, and can leave you feeling lonely, taken for granted, and loved conditionally — the feeling that you are only loved for what you provide and not for who you truly are. It is important to move to a place where you love yourself enough to know that you are worthy of being loved and cared for, and do not always have to be the one doing the giving. You feel you are worthy of receiving. It is vital to be "received": to share in a relationship that is built on respect and mutuality, where both persons have their needs met in healthy ways.

I have found it incredibly freeing to get to the place where I do not feel I have to rescue anyone or be anyone's saviour. I use the word saviour in this context for a specific reason. Many years ago I was talking with a friend about the dreams I had for the person who was my partner at the time. I had been strongly encouraging my partner to move her career in a specific direction and was experiencing a level of frustration because I felt she was not moving fast enough toward the actualization of the goal I had set for her. My friend listened intently, smiled, pointed to the crucifix affixed on my office wall, and said, "Joan, get down from the cross, we need the wood!" Message received loud and clear.

It is not uncharacteristic of therapists to remind couples that relationships are work. This is the therapist's way of encouraging them to be realistic in the expectations they have about one another and about their relationship. It is a way to remind couples that difficulties will inevitably present themselves, and to encourage them to pull together when things get challenging. In the case of unhealthy relationships, however, no matter how hard couples work at it there comes a time when — in the interests of the health of mind, body, and soul of both people — there is the need for the relationship to end. This is an extremely difficult situation, and to date I have not met even one person for whom this process has not been heart wrenching and devastating on some level. It is yet another reason why many people choose to remain in unhealthy relationships for so long — as an attempt, consciously or unconsciously, to try to avoid experiencing the depth of pain and sadness that accompanies the ending of a relationship. The reality is, however, that much of what we will ever learn about ourselves and others will be born from this very pain. Pain and loss are profound teachers. I can say this with the utmost confidence having been taught by both, time and time again in my own life.

As much as people do not want to invite pain and sadness into their lives, there are times when, in the interests of their own emotional health, they must walk away from a relationship. This relationship could be one shared with a romantic partner, a friend, or even a colleague. It is difficult leaving any relationship where we have invested ourselves emotionally, and in those times we are invited to befriend our woundedness and reap its wisdom. As we navigate our grief it is important to remind ourselves that even though the relationship did not last forever, the lessons we learn from it can. Knowing this in our depths can allow us to be open to the lessons the experience, however painful, has to offer. The new insights we gain will deepen us, and will inform and enrich future relationships.

Encouraging people to open up to their hurt and pain stands in opposition to a pain-defying culture that suggests people medicate and "numb out." It also flies in the face of the belief that there are ways to go under, around, or over emotional pain in our lives. The reality is that the only way to experience genuine healing is through sitting with and working through the pain. What a lost opportunity if we choose to emotionally "numb out" instead of accepting the invitation to open up, and letting the difficult parts of our lives be our greatest teachers.

When I was a little girl, it was a tradition that my family visited my grandparents' home every Sunday afternoon after church. My grandparents lived in an older home, and the windows contained the original thick glass. This meant that the view from the inside out was distorted. On a number of occasions, I stood at the front window searching for a section of glass that might give me a clear view to the outside. It seems from a young age I preferred clarity and desired to see things as they were, but now as a middle-aged woman I realize that clarity only comes with perspective and time. So too does the transition from pain and loss to healing and insight. It is not instantaneous; it takes time. We cannot get to a place of healing without naming our hurts. Pain needs its time, to allow us to discover the lessons it has to teach and to discern its meaning for our lives. In this way we gain clarity, and are able to be transformed from the inside out.

Part of the challenge during times of difficulty is being able to let go and surrender to the process. Those who have walked the painful path of broken relationships will tell you that surrendering is easier said than done because it involves handing over control, which demands tremendous trust. Some people struggle with the concept of surrendering because they think it means they are giving up, but in actuality it is not about giving up, it is about *giving over*. A big part of *giving over* involves letting go, which is essential to moving forward. One of my journal entries, written on the shores of Lake Huron, speaks to my desire to let go, and to my hope that freedom will ultimately come from surrendering: *So many feelings washing over me, like these waves washing over the rocks. I am trying to feel their depth, make sense of them, and yet not be overwhelmed by them…trying to trust enough to let go of the old to make room for the new…wanting to face the unfinished business of the past so I can enjoy a freer future.*

It is never easy to let go and surrender to the pain, because it is difficult to leap forward into darkness. It is human nature to want the surety of a safe landing before we jump, but I would humbly suggest that safe landings are not all they are cracked up to be. Perhaps deepening and wisdom come not from the sure-footed path at all, but from walking gently on the uneven ground into the darkness, moving forward, trusting in what is unclear, and having faith that things are unfolding as they are meant to. Wouldn't it be wonderful if we were able to get to the place where we could totally surrender and feel a sense of wonderment and curiosity about what is coming, versus always trying to control things?

Part of surrendering means, at times, having to let go of a relationship amidst the unfinished business that may still exist. Sometimes relationships must find closure even though unanswered questions and unresolved issues remain. Although hanging threads may linger, sometimes in the interests of our emotional health we must find a way to say goodbye so we can move forward. It is extremely difficult to find closure in these circumstances, but it is in our best emotional interest to do so, because we are not free to embrace the new if we are still clutching the old. We need to surrender, let go, and make room for new life to touch us.

I am a person who struggles in this area because I have a strong desire for harmony in my life, and this extends into my relationships. I prefer that all relationships come to an end amicably and be wrapped up with a neat and tidy bow. This is not realistic. Although some relationships are able to end amicably, in most cases the initial rupturing and dissolution of a relationship is extremely difficult and painful. Emotions like anger and hurt can run so deep that harmonious closure is impossible, at least for an initial period of time.

In some cases people look to the person they are separating from to find closure. It is extremely helpful if couples are able to do this for one another, and it often quickens the healing process. The reality is, however, that most couples are not capable of helping each other find closure because they have not yet found closure as individuals. In a very real sense, closure can only come from within; it is a gift we ultimately give ourselves. One of the things necessary for closure is to face the pain connected with the termination of a relationship head on. We need to name and feel our pain so we can let it go. Denying it delays the healing process. Having said that, I know it can be difficult to get in touch with our pain, especially if walls have been built. It takes a lot of trust to bring the walls down and let the sadness and hurt in. Sometimes we fear that if we lower our defences we will be overwhelmed by our feelings, but it is important to risk chipping away at the walls even if we must do it slowly, because although we think they are protecting us, they are only serving to encase our hearts and hold them captive.

Other people can be the conduit for removing the walls and enabling us to feel and deal with our hurt. Sometimes in seeing and experiencing the pain and suffering of others we are brought closer to seeing and feeling our own pain. I experienced this quite poignantly one day while spending time with my father. I was in my late forties at the time, and that decade of my life had been marked by a number of painful events. I had chosen to leave a ten-year relationship, I had moved out of a prolonged romantic relationship with someone who was unavailable, and I was continuing to watch my father die from Alzheimer's. What was unfolding in my outside life was deeply affecting my interior life, and many intense feelings were flowing in and out of my heart, most notably grief, hurt, sadness, and anger. Journaling was one of the creative ways I tried to access my feelings and cope during this emotionally challenging period of my life. The following journal entry reveals how fearful, desperate, and disoriented I felt: *Sometimes the darkness moves in without warning, demanding a time of reckoning. It is here that fear faces off with courage… and sometimes all you can do is pray for the light… I feel as if my soul has been torn to shreds, and my heart has lost its home.*

I kept busy in an attempt to avoid opening myself up to my feelings, feelings I feared ran so deep they would overwhelm me. It would be in a most surprising way that I would finally open up. I was out on a walk with my father, who at that time was deep in the throes of the devastating effects of Alzheimer's. Not long into the walk he came to an abrupt halt at a street corner. He turned and looked at me and I immediately saw the lost look in his eyes. I felt my father's panic as he frantically searched his mind for a clue about which way to turn to make his way back home. We stood still for a split second, and as I looked into his frightened eyes I felt an instant connection. His pain of memory loss intersected with my pain of lost love. There he stood feeling the betrayal of his mind, and there I stood feeling the betrayal of my heart. It was in that moment of experiencing my dad's pain and vulnerability that I was finally able to connect with my own suffering, and in essence find myself. It was a profound and powerful experience, one I will never forget. This soulful connection with my father marked the beginning of my opening up to the profound pain I had been carrying inside for a long time. It became an important step in my healing process.

I went on to share a number of similar experiences with my father throughout his illness. These profoundly intimate connections were graced moments, reminding me that other people are often gateways to the soul; midwives helping us birth our feelings so that we acknowledge them, learn their lessons, and ultimately find our peace. What a gift others can be in helping us connect with, name, and face our pain, so that hurt is not given the opportunity to paralyze and define us.

In reflecting on the painful relationships of my past it would be dishonest to say I enjoyed any part of what felt like a lengthy ride on the "hurting-go-round," but I am now able to see and appreciate the deepening and seasoning of self that arose from the depths of those dark nights of the soul. I am able to recognize that it is in meeting life, in all its struggle, that new insights and awareness are gained. I understand now how significant it was to my life's journey that I walked, and sometimes crawled, that very painful terrain. I know in the depths of my soul how important it was to choose to sit with the pain and heartache, rather than run from it, and I also know how supremely important it is to ask it, "What are you here to teach?"

Before we can sit with our pain there needs to be an element of trust that something positive will emerge from the pain. There needs to be hope that the suffering holds some meaning for our lives: *Bits of my soul are coming back to rest, bringing insight, wisdom and light…bringing me to a place I could not have imagined. I feel my heart returning to itself. I may never figure out why I was held there for so long…held within as much as from without… I just know it feels good to be building a future, instead of feeling stuck in a past.*

FORGIVENESS AND RESILIENCY

One of the things that help us let go and finally get closure is moving to a place in our hearts where we can forgive the people who have hurt us. Forgiveness is an important way we call our spirit back and feel whole again. From a forgiving place we are more able to recognize the good things that emerged from our relationship, in all its messiness and pain. A forgiving heart opens us up so we can feel gratitude for the valuable lessons learned, rather than expend energy rehashing the relationship and obsessively revisiting the hurt feelings attached to it.

In my experience, often the person we need to extend forgiveness to first is ourself, because we cannot give to others what we do not possess within. We have to forgive ourselves for making some of the choices we have made, such as choosing to move into relationships we suspected would not be healthy or life giving for us: *I am trying to forgive myself for having seen the many signs, yet out of my own neediness, not listening to them... for refusing to see them for what they were, and in this way denying them.*

It is naïve to say it is easy to forgive others, especially when we have been deeply hurt. Forgiving others takes time. Sometimes it helps to remind ourselves that all human beings have wounds, and that on any given day people do the best they can with what they have been given. We need to be reminded that most people do not set out to intentionally hurt other people. It can take many years to forgive someone who has devastated or deeply hurt us, to get to the place where we can say, "I forgive you for hurting me in the process of living out your humanity with its woundedness and imperfection." It takes most of us time and effort to forgive, but in the interests of our emotional health and well-being, it is important we make it a goal to do so.

Concentrating on who you have in your life rather than on who you do not have is another way of healing and moving through the pain of a break up. A spirit of gratitude for the people who remain in our lives and who continue to love, support, and sustain us helps bring healing and hope. The support of loved ones helps reassure us that the darkness will give way to light.

In the process of surrendering, letting go, and finally getting to a place where we feel gratitude for past relationships, things may happen that lead us to fear that we have taken a step backward. It is important to understand that unlike our chronological lives, our emotional lives are not linear. We may have times where we spiral and feel ourselves revisiting hurt-filled places. This does not mean we are losing ground in our healing process. These experiences are natural emotional tributaries that we need to flow with, rather than panic about. An example may be helpful here. My friend's ex-husband recently remarried. On the weekend of his remarriage, my friend found herself feeling some of the pain that was connected to the dissolution of her marriage to him many years previous. Initially she was taken aback by her feelings, asking herself if she was moving backwards. Upon reflection, however, she was able to identify her feelings as normal and natural rather than indicators that she was slipping back into that time of profound hurt in her life. She was able to understand them as thoughts and feelings that simply needed acknowledgement so they could be sent on their way. What some people identify as setbacks may well be normal reactions caused by the emotional investment of the past intersecting with the concrete circumstances of the present. For some people, experiences like my friend's provide the necessary final look back that allows them to turn and move forward once and for all. Last looks can be painful but they can also be incredibly freeing, because they make room for new life, providing hope for the future.

In experiencing first-hand the pain of leaving a relationship, and in observing the experiences of others who are doing the same, I am struck by how resilient human beings are. We are often much stronger then we believe ourselves to be, and this is tremendously encouraging. As I think about resilience, I go back in time to the backyard of the family home where I grew up. In middle of the yard stood a huge weeping willow tree that was quite majestic. Not so majestic were some of the tiny inhabitants lodged in its branches; my parents referred to them as "beer bugs." These black beetles were indiscriminate in invading any beverage left unattended, and over the years they became increasingly annoying to my mother and father, who would find them swimming unabated in their refreshments. Not surprisingly, there came a day when a decision was made that Mr. Willow would weep his last. My brother-in-law and his trusty chain saw were summoned to do the (literally) dirty deed. One day I returned home from school to find willowy wooden remnants scattered on the ground near a hefty stump where the tree had once stood. Although I understood why the tree's days had been numbered, I felt sad seeing its dismembered parts lying aimlessly on the ground, for as a young girl I had spent many afternoons cradled in its branches. Over the next few days all the branches were toted away until all that remained was the stump. The willow's massive roots were deeply entrenched, so instead of having the entire backyard unearthed to remove the stump, my parents opted to leave it where it was. It was less than a month later that I witnessed several green sprouts staging a silent rebellion by boldly poking their heads out from the top of the stump. I smiled at their tenacity. I think of that old stump today because it reminds me of the resiliency of the human spirit. We grow in love, and experience the heartache of love lost, but with time our hearts sprout anew!

There is no denying that moving out of a relationship is an incredibly painful experience, but wisdom can be gained with every goodbye as our understanding of self deepens. If we take the time to reflect and learn from our relationships, we grow in awareness, become more conscious, and ultimately live more freely. It is important to resist the strong urge to move quickly from one relationship to another; this is often motivated by loneliness and the need to distract ourselves from the pain. Instead, we need to take time to harvest the lessons that are ripe for the picking.

One of the first questions I suggest people ask someone they are considering moving into a new relationship with is, "What are some important insights you have learned about *yourself* from past relationships?" If, upon reflection, the person cannot answer that question, or answers it by blaming past partners for all the things that went wrong in their relationships, I would suggest one proceed with caution...or run quick! Emotionally healthy people are able to identify and own their part in where past relationships have broken down. They understand the need to continue to grow as an individual, and value self-awareness as a contributing factor to the engagement in healthier relationships moving forward.

All things being said, it is important to acknowledge that no individual is perfect, nor does a perfect relationship exist. What does exist is our ability to be intentional and committed to growing in consciousness, which enables us to love ourselves more deeply, and others more freely. In this place, we are able to embrace the fullness of what relationships have to offer and teach, amidst *the loving, the learning, and the letting go.*

After much heartache and pain, came a new day and a new way of being...what began as grief, anger, sadness, and loneliness, transformed into humility, grace, and gratitude.

Deepening Your Life…

Do you think it is true that we are often drawn (unconsciously) to others out of our own need? Do you see others as you need *to see them versus seeing them for who they truly are? Have you had someone project their needs onto you? What was that experience like and how did it impact your relationship?*

In what ways are you consciously striving to become a whole person, so that you have no need to look for people to complete you?

Have you ever played the role of rescuer, or been the one being rescued in relationship? What did it feel like? What impact did playing this role have on your relationship?

What are some of the positive insights you have learned about yourself from past relationships? If you cannot identify any, why do you think this is so?

Do you find it hard to let go and surrender in times of hurt and pain? If yes, what do you think gets in the way of being able to let go?

Why is it a healthy choice, at the level of mind, body, and soul, to feel and express the many emotions that naturally arise with the termination of a relationship (e.g., anger, sadness, hurt, betrayal, and pain)? What are some concrete things you do to provide an avenue to express your emotions?

Have you ever connected with your own pain or struggle through the pain and suffering of another? If yes, when? What did you learn from this important connection?

Is there someone in your life you need to offer forgiveness? If yes, what is keeping you from doing so?

Name a time in your life where you showed resilience. What did this experience teach you about yourself?

CHAPTER FIVE

Who Will Drive My Soul?

NURTURED BY NATURE

I am guessing that, like me, you have had the experience of driving alone in your car listening to music and being grabbed by the lyric of a song. It might be a phrase or even just a word that catches your ear, but something interrupts your thinking and gives you pause for reflection. Perhaps you have heard this same lyric a number of times before, but at that moment you are compelled by the words because they resonate with where you are in your life. I have these experiences often, and in some cases the lyrics don't linger just for a day, but for years. Such is the case with the line of a song, by the Canadian-born artist *Lights*, which poses the question *Who will drive my soul?* I believe the reason this lyric continues to speak to me is that this question has ongoing significance for my life: I come back to it time and time again. I have chosen therefore to pay attention not only to the question itself, but to how I answer it.

Who *does* drive my soul? Do I allow my soul to be driven by the world, which is motivated more times than not by egocentricity and a focus on the attainment of power, profit, status, and prestige? Is my soul driven by the people around me, some of whom want me to act a certain way in order to meet their needs? Or, is my soul driven by personal integrity, directing who I am and how I want to live and be in the world?

As you can see, a seemingly innocuous lyric presents quite a challenge! I like to believe I am the one driving my soul, but I know at times I allow myself to be relegated to the passenger seat — for example, when I succumb to the seduction of the competitive, individualistic, and materialistic world around me. It takes conscious effort to drive one's soul while living in a culture that often encourages that which is soul defying. There are a number of ways I try to consciously *drive my soul* and limit the time spent in the passenger seat, and that is the focus of this chapter.

Having a graduate degree in theology does very little to help me articulate what I mean by the word soul. Dusting off a few university textbooks would allow me to pull together a decent overview of what some of the greatest theologians have understood soul to mean, but I am more interested in how soul is *experienced* than in how it is defined. As I have come to experience it, soul is the place where we touch our divine essence and gain a clearer glimpse of the mystery within. It is a place of knowingness that defies description or comprehension, a sacred space where we hear the gentle whisperings of love beyond all understanding, and are assured that all is unfolding as it is meant to. The soul is the place where wisdom drips.

Soul is a noun that has the resonance of a verb, because it correlates with an action: living soulfully. Soulfulness means having a deep connection within — feeling grounded and "at home" with self. It is seeing and experiencing tenderness and beauty, and being passionately engaged with life. It is revelling in stillness, quiet, and solitude, all of which allow us to hear the echo from within. It is the humility and the compassionate presence that enable us to respect and honour others' truths as we name our own. It is embracing our darkness and its power to challenge, teach, and inform. Soulfulness is experiencing our own goodness and grace. It is felt abundance.

Communing with one's soul is a sacred experience, and once we connect with our soul we want to nurture, protect, and be present to it in an ongoing way. Nurturing and protecting one's soul is at the essence of the question, *who will drive my soul*? People may differ in the ways they nurture their souls and sustain soulfulness, but *how* they do it is less important than the commitment to doing so.

One of the significant ways I nurture my soul is by creating frequent opportunities to be immersed in nature, which allows my soul the opportunity to breathe and speak. It is in nature that I experience deep peace, for it is in her embrace that my soul comes home and finds rest. Away from the frenetic pace of work and daily life, which serve to crowd the soul, nature provides a much-needed invitation to stop and be still. Nature possesses restorative properties; it is a soothing balm for the soul. The solitude and stillness nature provides allows me to hear the whispering of earth's primal beat — a soulful cadence that syncopates with the life I feel surging within me, reminding me that I am part of the earth not separate from it.

One of the most soul-nurturing experiences for me is being in and around water. It is not a coincidence that I was born under the sign Pisces, the Latin word for fish! I find water to be regenerative, which is why I try to spend as much time as possible out in my sea kayak. I feel an instant calm wash over me each time I sit down in her and launch out into the water. Some of my most soulful moments have been experienced from the cockpit of a kayak. One such moment occurred a number of years ago while I was sea kayaking in Alaska. A friend and I had joined up with a paddling company operating out of a small town called Petersburg. This particular trip was nine days in duration, with time divided between two base camps. One camp was situated where we could kayak around icebergs and "bergie bits" (iceberg pieces that dislodge and float on the ocean's surface); the other camp was located on the shores of Frederick Sound, where we would kayak with humpback whales. It was on day four of the trip that our group of nine was out paddling in the middle of Frederick Sound. Someone spotted whale spray far out on the horizon, and in hopes of gaining a closer look the group began paddling vigorously in the spray's direction. I chose to follow in behind at a gentler pace so I could take in the sights and sounds along the way. This particular day was uncharacteristically warm and sunny for Alaskan weather, so at one point as the others continued to paddle in pursuit of the whales, I stopped briefly, took my paddle out of the water, and set my face to the sun. The warmth of the sun's rays felt comforting and invigorating, so I held this position for a few minutes, totally immersed in the experience. As I went to put my paddle back into the water I heard the unmistakable sound of the blow of a whale. It seemed quite close. As I turned my head in the direction of the sound, I saw the trailing mist of a whale's blow, fifty yards to the right of where I was. My eyes keenly scanned the area. I saw nothing on the watery surface for a number of minutes, but just as I was about to resume paddling, it happened: To my right, now only about twenty-five yards away, rising slightly above the water, were two grey humps side by side, one bigger than the other. I watched intently as a mother humpback, a calf close at her side, swam by. At no time did the calf emerge, but the mother quietly surfaced and gracefully poked her head up out of the water. In that split second the whale and I met eye to eye. I had never sat that still in a kayak in my life! I was paralyzed, not out of fear, but out of absolute amazement. It is difficult to describe the experience except to say it was a mystical encounter that literally took my breath away. I had never experienced *awesome* in such an embodied way. In meeting eye to eye, the whale and I shared an intimate exchange. There was a *knowingness* between us, a shared nod to the beauty of life by two vastly different creatures… yet perhaps not so different at all.

At the beginning of the paddling trip, the guide had instructed us to yell out and point our paddles in the direction of any whales spotted. The intent was to ensure the entire group could enjoy all whale sightings. I was so taken in and moved by the experience, I could not have found the voice to yell even if I had wanted to. The whole encounter felt unbelievable and surreal. It was as if I was outside the experience, looking in as it unfolded. It took me a while to fathom that I had shared communion with such a magnificent creature.

After this experience I sat for a minute processing what had occurred. Looking back, I am grateful I was unable to call out to the others. The encounter I had with the whale was such a sacred moment that to have yelled out, and undoubtedly incited a flurry of paddles and kayaks in the whale's direction, would have cheapened the experience. That afternoon at our shore lunch I told the story of what had happened. Not one person believed me, including the guide, who said that since we were all within two hundred yards of one another, more of us would have heard the whale's blow, seen the mist, and heard the sound that would have undoubtedly occurred had a whale actually plunged its enormous head above water. The teasing from the group was relentless, continuing for the duration of lunch. I just sat and smiled. I knew what I had seen, and more importantly, I knew what I had experienced. It was a soulful exchange that I will never forget.

The eye-to-eye meeting with the whale would not be the only profound experience I had on that trip. On the evening before our final day, a few of us asked our guide if she would be willing to take us out for one last paddle the next morning, before we had to abandon our kayaks, board a motor boat, and make our way back to Petersburg. The guide graciously agreed but informed us that we would need to get up at 5:00 a.m. in order to fit in the paddle before departure time. And so the next morning, well before sunrise, five of us hauled our bedraggled bodies out of our sleeping bags, emerged slowly from our tents, and poured our half-awake selves into our kayaks. Before we launched from shore the guide suggested we do a silent paddle, which entailed paddling without talking to one another for the full two hours out on the water. The extroverts in the group (that would include me!) were more than a bit apprehensive about the call to prolonged silence, but eventually everyone agreed to the plan.

What a deeply spiritual experience the silent paddle proved to be. That morning everything was tranquil and fresh. The water was completely calm. Each of us embraced the stillness as we quietly paddled out into the morning mist, which soon enveloped us like a hazy curtain. Every one paddled gingerly; no one wanted to disrupt the serene spirit of the experience. We were totally captured by the beautiful seascape, and our ears were thrilled by the intermittent blows of humpback whales far out at sea — their steamy exhalations welcoming us to a new day. We were all conscious of allowing one another space to find our own special pocket where we could just "be" in the moment. At times I chose to simply sit still in my kayak and revel in the purity and peacefulness, wishing somehow there was a way to capture the feeling in a bottle, so that once home I could release the cap and enjoy the calm over and over again.

Sadly, far too soon, the two-hour paddle came to an end, and it was time to head to shore. With less than fervent strokes, each of us made our way in; no one wanted the soulful paddle to end. We continued in silence as we disembarked and removed the gear from our kayaks. We simply smiled over at each other. We had shared something special; we had experienced solitude together. As the other paddlers made their way back to camp, I sat on shore and made an effort to describe my experience. Fully cognizant of the limitations of adequately capturing its profundity in words, I forged a humble attempt:

Stillness

Nature envelops me
All around I am held
My soul feels a freedom
I cannot explain
I experience a knowingness
that things will be okay

Silence

Only the sound of paddles
making gentle strokes through still waters
Carrying us forward with grace…
With each stroke
I am brought home to myself

Alone

Out in the open
I lift my paddle and slowly glide to a stop
Pointing my kayak toward the mountains
I see the mist rising…
I close my eyes
Tiny liquid beads come to rest on my face
A soggy kiss of nature
I am content

Being

A whale blows in the distance
A serene soulful sound
In this moment
I am able to surrender it all…
And realize this is all I need

To the whales…

O Majestic Ones
You generously share
your liquescent playground
Letting us in on your one and only secret…
That it is in letting go
that we are most free

It was truly a morning I will never forget, and one I wish could have lasted a lifetime. It is my hope that everyone has something in their lives that connects them to their soul, to beauty, and to the sustaining nature of God's creation, as kayaking does for me. We all need something that helps us stay in the driver's seat and drive our soul.

THE INNER SEASONS OF OUR LIVES

You do not have to go paddling in Alaska or engage in an outdoor adventure to connect with nature and benefit from its soul-sustaining powers. God plays "show and tell" everyday via the created world. All we need do is show up, breathe it in, and be open to its healing properties. It could be as simple as taking a moment to admire the beauty of a tree whose leaves generously provide shelter and shade. Or making the choice to lie still in bed an extra minute to enjoy listening to the rain pouring down its spirited tap dance on the roof. It could be taking the time to look up and marvel at the beauty of the pastel swirls in a summer sky, imagining their sweeping patterns as the work of an artist painting with total abandon. It could involve taking a moment to stand on a beach paying homage to the fading sun as it gracefully bows down towards the water and bids adieu to the day. Nature is always ready and willing to feed our soul, but often we choose busy-ness over presence towards the world around us, and in doing so we fail to reap nature's ability to soothe and restore.

A very powerful way nature offers us the opportunity to nurture our soul is through the cycling of the seasons. The changing seasons create a context for reflection upon the movements occurring in our lives. As nature moves through its cycle of birth, death, and new life, so too do we, both literally and metaphorically. As a resident of Ontario I experience four distinct seasons as nature moves from the biting chill of winter to the radiant light of spring, and from the sustaining warmth of summer to the darkening days of fall.

The seasonal changes unfolding in the outside world mirror the transformations occurring in our inner world. Like the natural world around us, we experience different seasons in our lives. Our life experiences of winter often include times of loss, pain, struggle, separation, betrayal, and disappointment. Accompanying such experiences can be feelings of anger, fear, sadness, hurt, doubt, guilt, anxiety, and disillusionment. Our winter experiences disturb and disorient us, leaving us feeling abandoned, hopeless, lost, and alone. At these times we lack clarity about where life is leading us, and we find this unsettling. We are left feeling emotionally paralyzed and confused. Yet, during our disoriented state, winter dares ask us to be patient and still…and to wait… and trust in dormancy, the place where on the surface all seems dead and forgotten, yet underneath life is stirring and regenerating, and very much thriving: *I love the quiet of a gentle winter snowfall as it blankets the earth, readying it for things to come. Life takes respite… hibernating and regrouping for the journey ahead.*

Our winter asks us to trust in the assurance of spring, where new life will emerge from our pain, and be incarnated in a deepened awareness of self. If we are able to wait out winter's darkness we will discover that our trust in spring has not been in vain, for spring does indeed come:

Spring is here…

Sun illuminates our morning
The pastel sky bids us good night
And all around life reminds us once again
that it is alive, and all shall be well

Trees eagerly unfold their offering
Green buds exuberant with potential
Magnificent roots planted firmly in the earth
taking a stand for creation

And so it is with the spring of our lives…

A time for graced renewal
A time to turn our face once again
toward the sun which has always been
Yet now makes itself more fully known

Like the emerging shoots and buds on the trees, our spring experiences invite us to new growth by challenging us to leave the security of the familiar, and embrace the new. We are encouraged to change and deepen, and in this way discover new ways of living, loving, and being.

Spring marks a season of possibility for our inner lives as it calls us to recognize and develop our potential. Nurturing our potential is an important part of growing our souls. How sad it would be to turn our backs on our potential, much like refusing to water a seedling that has the innate capacity for growth. We need to identify our God-given potential and ask ourselves if we have watered it enough! Some people search for their potential *outside* themselves. In essence, they look to others for validation, thus moving the locus of control from self to others, and in so doing give others the power to define them. We need to resist the temptation to hand our personal power over to others; instead, we need to recognize and develop our potential. Spring reminds us that what we need for personal growth is found within. It asks us to place trust in ourselves, in our intuition, and in our innate wisdom, because all emanate from a deep place of knowingness: our soul.

Spring reminds us that conditions must be right for growth to occur. Just as rain is needed to moisten the earth and provide fertile soil from which new life can emerge, so too our inner life needs fertile conditions in which to grow. Essential to inner growth is having an open mind and heart, which allow us to challenge ourselves and gain new understandings. In order to be open, our ego must be secure enough in itself to enable us to let down our defences and risk vulnerability. In this place we are able to be receptive to the perspectives, life experiences, and wisdom of others. Insular thinking is always paralyzing to personal growth. In making room in our minds and hearts for other ways of seeing and experiencing the world, our narrow and limited perspectives are stretched, and our consciousness expanded. We broaden the walls of our existence when we learn from one another. Opening ourselves up to others provides balance and moves us toward deeper integration of self.

Amidst the call to personal growth and renewal, spring reminds us to be patient with ourselves. As a teenager, I recall having a conversation with a mentor who said that people are most often hardest on themselves. In order to illustrate his point he took a pencil and drew a tiny dot in the middle of a white page. He then asked me to describe what I saw. I told him I saw a tiny black dot. He smiled and said that most people gave that same answer. He suggested that as human beings our tendency is to focus on the small back dot, representing our inadequacies and shortcomings, rather than seeing the predominance of white on the page, symbolizing our goodness, which far surpasses our faults. I share this story as a way of suggesting that self-improvement and personal growth are admirable goals, but while focusing on the ways we need to improve, we also need to recognize our inherent goodness and celebrate the joy we bring to those around us. It is important that we heed the liberating call of springtime, which reminds us that everything needs time to grow and to "season," and that alongside the desire for self-development, we need patience and kindness towards self. Just as the movement from seedling to flowering plant is not instantaneous, transformation in our inner world does not happen overnight. All growth takes time. Spring reminds us that growing our souls is an ongoing process and encourages us to be gentle with ourselves.

In spring we marvel at the emerging beauty of the natural world around us, but do we ever stop to marvel at our own beauty and goodness? Spring reminds us that there is absolutely nothing to be gained from downplaying our essence, suppressing the unique contribution we are called to share with the world. The blossoming flowers and glowing fields do not apologize for their radiance, nor should we. Like spring's array of beauty, whose intention it is to be enjoyed by all, our beauty is to be celebrated and delighted in too!

Increased opportunities for learning and growth continue to present themselves as the cycle of nature continues and spring gives way to summer. It is in summer that the promises of spring come to fruition, and what began emerging and budding in spring can now be seen in its full regalia. Trees, shrubs, and grasses showcase their spectrum of green, and flowers are plentiful, colourful, and vibrant. Petal heads torque toward the sun that nurtures and sustains them. In summer the earth shows off, as creation emerges in all its blooming glory! Summer is a welcome season for the earth, which has cycled its way through the long chill of winter and the slow thaw of spring.

So too is summer is a welcome season for our inner lives, for that which was long hidden in the darkness and depths of winter, and which was hoped for in spring, now becomes manifest. Our trusting in the unknown pays off as we experience the rewards of waiting and trusting in that which we could not see. Whether our summer experience involves getting to the other side of a prolonged period of struggle, being able to finally feel forgiveness in our heart for a person who has deeply wounded us, or having any other experience of our soul's movement forward, in summer we experience an inner freedom previously unknown.

Summer ushers in "Aha!" moments where seemingly disparate pieces of our lives come together, and confusion gives way to clarity. In looking back we come to understand the purpose of our suffering and discover its meaning. We gain the awareness that our difficult and dark experiences have been the very thing needed to stretch us so we might be transformed, healed, and made whole. In summer we come to see that our lives are made richer by our winters, falls, and springs, which ultimately bring us into the light where wisdom is gained by staying the course.

In summer we feel a level of joy and lightness of being and are grateful for all that has come to be. Reviving waters flow, as the wellspring of our soul, parched and sucked dry by the wear and tear of life, gets welcome replenishment. Summer provides the much-needed opportunity for us to play and be creative, which brings balance and renews our spirit. In summer we come to know that all is well and is unfolding as it is meant to.

Summer is a high-spirited season full of light and energy. There is the temptation to want to live there forever, but this is impossible. The unfolding events in our lives will naturally propel us out of summer. There are people, nonetheless, who make an attempt to live in summer forever; this illusion is supported by North American culture, which tells us that we can. Evidence of "buy in" to this illusion is all around us. Some people spend exorbitant amounts of money on plastic surgery in a futile attempt to stay young. Others move quickly from one relationship to another in hopes of permanently capturing the thrill of the infatuation stage — precluding them from ever attaining any depth of emotional intimacy. Some people incur major debt in order to live in the fast lane. Still others develop addictions in an attempt to numb out and avoid their "winters." No matter the means used, the reality remains that it is impossible to live in summer forever. Nor should we, for it is healthy to acknowledge and accept that all things need to surrender. It is through our immersion in each individual season that we learn to let go, wait, grow, and ripen. It is from full participation in the cycle of our inner seasons that insight and gratitude flow, for if not for the surrender of fall and the darkness of winter, how would we appreciate the hope of spring and the renewal of summer? Each season needs to be embraced, for each has unique lessons and wisdom to offer.

As the natural world continues its cycle, the long sunny days of summer surrender to the shorter, darker days of fall.

Now it is time for the abundant gifts of the earth, grown during summer, to be gathered and harvested. Likewise, in our inner lives it is time to give thanks for the grace of summer, and to walk with trust into the fields where our hearts can be tilled. In fall, the season of surrender, we are invited to sift the wheat and chaff of our lives and unclutter our souls. We are offered the opportunity to discern what we should hang on to, nurture, and move forward with, and what we should surrender because it no longer serves our soul. The wheat — lessons learned and insights gained — we are encouraged to treasure and store in our minds and hearts, where it can continue to guide and inform us, serving as steppingstones leading us forward. The chaff — thoughts and feelings that limit us — we are called to let go. They have had their time, and perhaps even served their purpose, but now only weigh us down. In fall we acknowledge their limitations and let them go so that we can live more fully and more freely.

In reflecting on the call to surrender I think of my beloved dog, Cody. Sadly she is now deceased, but for over fifteen years as I sat in my favourite chair to read or journal, she would jump up, create a nesting spot on my lap, and instantly fall asleep. She would lie there peacefully by the hour, totally given over to the experience, surrendered and content. Intermittently I would look down at her and envy her ability to completely let go and trust. I would ponder why at times it was so difficult for me to surrender. In observing her contented state I would be affirmed in my belief that animals are incredibly soulful beings with much to teach us.

Surrendering is hard, so it is not surprising that many people resist letting go. It can be difficult to let dead things truly die. In the fall, like many people, I enjoy looking at the changing colours of the leaves. Every year late in the season I am struck by the same reoccurring image of a single leaf clinging to the branch of a tree, when the tree's other leaves have all surrendered to the wind and fallen crumpled to the ground. I find myself captivated by that one leaf hanging precariously by a thread on an otherwise barren branch. I ask myself: Is this leaf brave or foolish? Should it be admired for its bold stand-off against the wind, or pitied for its stubborn spirit that has it clinging desperately to a lifeless branch — looking for sustenance where none is to be found? It makes me think about my life. Are there times when I dangle and whirl about, stubbornly clinging to something or someone when I should be letting go? Are there times I self-sabotage by looking for sustenance in the wrong place, and in doing so set myself up for disappointment? If yes, why do I do this? Why is it so difficult at times to surrender and trust that there is meaning and purpose in letting go and "falling to the ground"?

On some level it is human nature to want to cling to the known, even if it no longer serves us. Without the assurance of a sturdy branch in front to grasp, it is difficult to surrender our hold on the branch we cling to. Stepping into the darkness and living with uncertainty is never comfortable, but the season of fall assures us that there is much to be gained by taking risks and surrendering, because it is in letting go that we create room to discover new things about ourselves, others, and the world around us. It is in giving over that we experience increased freedom and insight. Letting go becomes the conduit for *letting in* and allows that which tied our soul down to be released so it can make way for new life. New life shows itself through our participation in different experiences, which broaden our perspectives and lead us to increased awareness. In fall we come to understand that, like that leaf, there are times when we need to draw on our resilience in order to persevere and fight the good fight, but other times when we need to *let go* so we can *let in*. It is important to spend time discerning when we should hang on and when we should let go.

The season of fall calls us to surrender the hurts we have carried in our hearts for a long time. This includes making peace with the people in our lives who have caused us the most heartache. Sometimes we refuse to let go of our pain, thinking that withdrawing forgiveness is a way to punish others. But the truth of the matter is that when we fail to forgive others it is ourselves that we hold captive. Like a poison dart aimed at self, refusing to forgive is punishment turned inward. It is toxic and hardens our heart, rendering us inaccessible. Withholding forgiveness ultimately sabotages our soul. Fall invites us to clothe ourselves in humility and acknowledge that we too fail at times and need forgiveness. It asks us to let go of our expectation that human beings be perfect, and extend to others the same emotional concessions we require when we ourselves make mistakes and hurt people. We are asked to adopt the belief that people are fundamentally good, and are worth far more than the worst decision they will ever make. We are reminded that, for the most part, everyone does the best they can with the emotional resources they possess, or lack.

One of the ways surrendering is made easier is through belief in an Abiding Presence. It is less difficult to surrender if we know and trust that we are being guided by grace. *Sophia*, divine wisdom, is Abiding Presence for me. When I find myself resisting and holding on — most often due to fear and feelings of insecurity — it is my trust in *Sophia* that enables me to finally let go. I am immensely grateful for her faithfulness and support.

She is wisdom incarnate, and I take comfort in her care. In times when you are asked to let go and surrender, call upon that which gives you strength and support.

The season of surrender eventually comes to an end as fall gives way to winter, and the cycle of nature begins anew. Similarly, the cycle of growth continues in our inner lives as we persevere in our winters, hope in our springs, revel in our summers, and surrender in our falls. In saying "yes" to the call of each season, we become ripened in wisdom.

For everything there is a season (Ecclesiastes 3:1)

STILLNESS AND SILENCE

The cycling of the seasons provides a rich context for connecting us with our inner lives, thus enabling us to grow in consciousness and drive our souls. Nature also offers the opportunity to stop and be still, which is essential to feeding our souls. It is an understatement to say that the hectic pace at which most of us move is crippling for mind, body, and soul. Running from task to task has become the "new normal," leaving us feeling emotionally drained, physically exhausted, and in some cases totally burned out. I was driving home from work one Friday night, and while sitting at a stoplight I noticed the remains of a suet bag swinging from a tree branch. Birds had pecked the bag right down to the string, and not a single seed remained. I empathized with that straggly remnant as it blew aimlessly in the wind, for it felt as if all week long people had been pecking away at me too! I sat there feeling exhausted. I had nothing left to give; I had no more "seeds" to share. I had nourished others but had neglected to feed myself. Inside I felt like that scruffy string blowing in the breeze! I realized in that moment how desperately I needed to stop and find solitude, quiet time alone to replenish the waters of my well of well-being. I do not think my experience is unique. Today, perhaps more than ever, we all need time for stillness and silence. How else will our soul have a chance to catch its breath and speak its wisdom?

If we are to keep our soul a priority we need to create time to be still. We must be intentional about creating time for solitude, because there are more than enough distractions willing to move in and fill up our days…and our lives! Some people argue that they are far too busy and cannot possibly find time to be still. I do not pass judgment on them, for I do not walk in their shoes, nor do I live their lives. I would humbly suggest, however, that the busier our lives are the more essential it is that we find time for stillness, which serves to ground and restore us. If we do not take time to connect with our soul, our lives begin to feel scattered and meaningless. Taking time for soulful connection is essential for health of mind, body, and spirit. It is crucial in helping us discern where we are meant to move in both our inner and outer worlds. My life is deeply enriched by taking time to nourish my soul, and for this reason, building in time for stillness has become one of my "non-negotiables."

Stillness creates space for clarity to emerge. When sitting quietly we give ourselves the opportunity to clear foggy thinking. Quiet time enables us to step back and avoid drowning in a sea of fragmented thoughts and emotions, which leave us feeling twisted and torn inside. Stillness offers a time of release by providing our soul an opportunity to exhale. In this exhalation, what has been ruminating within, most likely at an unconscious level, gets a chance to come forward. When our thoughts and feelings are in front of us we are able to look at them, name them, and begin to make sense of them. This is essential if we are to move toward deeper integration. It is through ensuring time for stillness and exhalation that we feed our soul rather than deplete it… and in this way keep ourselves in the driver's seat.

Having a sense of purpose and meaning is also essential if we are to drive our soul. Again, stillness plays an important role because it is in times of quiet and solitude that we give ourselves space to reflect on our experiences and discern their significance for our lives. The speed at which we move through life can result in our mindlessly going through the motions, never making the important connections needed for the increased awareness and insight that is so essential to finding meaning. In creating time for stillness and reflection we grant ourselves the opportunity to rediscover our purpose, so that we can move forward with increased passion and vision.

Some individuals find it helpful to establish a special place where they can physically go to be quiet and still. This becomes sacred space for them, where their soul has a chance to breathe. I have a few such places, but my favourite is found along the shoreline of Lake Huron, where on a less populated section of beach there are a number of huge rocks nestled together. I have come to call this grouping of rocks my prayer rocks, because I perch upon them to think, reflect, unwind, meditate, and journal. It is here that I reconnect within and revisit self. Every spring, for over twenty years, I have made a pilgrimage down the beach to find these rocks. They have become old weathered friends, and I feel a sense of "coming home" as I walk the shoreline and see them draw near. They provide me with a place to just "be:" *How I love these rocks, my sacred place, where Sophia plays in the waves and invites me into the dance.*

My prayer rocks are stalwarts of strength — solid, dependable friends, steady and sure, grounding me and enabling me to let go. They are a place of release for me, and their rugged surfaces are no strangers to my tears. It is here that I allow them to flow most freely: *Each tearful release, a ritual… tiny droplets plummet and become subsumed in the lake below; a holy communion — the cry of my soul mingling with creation and its ancient promise that all shall be well… through this tearful participation I am one with creation and Creator.*

Not all people are comfortable with stillness and silence, which is why some individuals go out of their way to stay busy. Some people find it incredibly difficult to just "be." For a number of years, I planned and facilitated retreats for leaders in my school board. As part of the retreat experience, people were asked to spend short periods of time alone in silence. On every retreat, without fail, at least one participant, often more, would share with me the struggle they had honouring the quiet time. People would openly confess that they had actively sought out others to talk to after only a few minutes. It always amazed me how the restless participants managed to find one another!

If we find it difficult to sit still and be quiet, it would serve us well to ask why? Is there something we fear will happen if we stop and just "be"? Is there something or someone we are trying to avoid facing? Are we afraid of letting our soul speak? Do we fear the changes our soul might be calling us to make? Our soul always desires that we be whole, so no matter how hard we try to elude its call, it will keep tapping, and will eventually begin banging on our door until we choose to wake up to something that needs acknowledgement and care. If the knock of our soul goes unheeded it will simply find a way to knock louder, sometimes through physical illness. Some people invest valuable time attempting to outrun the knock of their souls, but their efforts are in vain. What we try to avoid will always catch up with us. It is in our best interest emotionally, spiritually, and physically, to stop and listen.

Stillness and silence are truth bearers, lanterns bringing all things out of the darkness and into the light. In stopping and allowing ourselves to be still, we create space for the demons that have set up camp within to come out into the open. It can feel incredibly scary to come face to face with them, but addressing them head on is the only way we stay in the driver's seat and drive our soul. The demons in our lives will not magically disappear or go away on their own; they will keep rearing their indomitable heads until we face them. Thankfully the rewards of facing our issues are many, and it is important to trust in that while working them through.

The issues people need to face and integrate will vary. Some people's issues run deep, and extend back to pain connected with their family of origin. Other people carry hurts they have tried to bury, from past relationships. Still others live with the profoundly painful memories of emotional, physical, or sexual abuse, which in some cases they have kept secret for years. For me, it was denying that I was gay. Regardless of the type of issue, at some point we must find the courage to face our demons when they step forward. In facing them we take their power away. This emotional showdown can feel overwhelming and frightening, so it is important to invite others to walk alongside us. Drawing on the support, expertise, and care of other people strengthens us for the journey.

As we gain experience working through the issues in our lives, we develop increased confidence and trust in self. We begin to welcome quiet time as an important opportunity to hear the call of our soul, and we grow to value our "checking in with self" time. We no longer fear silence or times of stillness, because we know beyond a doubt that we can handle whatever feelings might surface. We know that facing our issues, as difficult as they can be, is the only way we move to the other side of our pain and find healing and emotional freedom. We recognize how good it feels to stop running. And, perhaps for the first time, we come to trust our soul.

GRATITUDE AND STAYING AMAZED

Another way we nurture and drive our soul is by feeling gratitude for our lives and all we have been given. Feeling gratitude is a powerful way to stay in the driver's seat. A number of years ago I watched a car crash survivor being interviewed on television. He suggested people adopt an "attitude of gratitude" and shared how coming face to face with death had helped him truly appreciate life. He shared his hope that people will not need horrendous accidents to feel thankful for their loved ones and the many gifts in their lives. His words made me think about how often I take my life for granted, including my loved ones, my health, and my job. Not long after hearing this interview, I designated a table in my living room as a gratitude centre. Upon it I regularly place cards, pictures of loved ones, and other special items, so that when I walk by I am reminded to give thanks for the many blessings in my life. In the middle of my special table is a clay container, which I call my gratitude jar. Beside it sits a pen and small pieces of paper. When so inspired I go over, write down what I feel most grateful for on that particular day, and place the paper into the gratitude jar. Every few months I light a candle, sit down in my favourite chair, take out the pieces of paper, and slowly read them over. As I place them back into the jar I say a prayer for the person whose name is recorded, and give thanks for the blessing they are in my life.

There are many ways to remind ourselves to have an "attitude of gratitude." Having a gratitude table or gratitude jar is but one way to give thanks. Any practice that helps you develop a spirit of gratitude is invaluable. What is most important is to create a ritual that holds meaning for *you*. Our soul expands when we have an "attitude of gratitude," because when we are deeply grateful for our lives and our loved ones, our hearts feel full and we are inspired to use some of our energy to support and nurture others. This outward movement of energy helps us avoid self-absorption.

Part of feeling grateful is having an appreciation for the simple things in life. I gain peculiar enjoyment from reading automobile bumper stickers (I am sure this is now considered distracted driving!), and of those I've seen over the years, two stand out as my all-time favourites. One of them has absolutely nothing to do with this discussion, but I share it here anyway in hopes of bringing a smile to your face. It reads, "Jesus is coming…look busy!" God help us if we do not keep a sense of humour! The other sticker, which ties directly in with the topic of gratitude, reads, "Stay Amazed!" This message is profound in its simplicity. It speaks to the importance of staying curious and keeping a sense of wonder. "Stay Amazed!" is countercultural in a world that honours the rational over the intuitive, and that analyzes all things in an attempt to understand, categorize, and control. No doubt this is why most adults have to consciously work at staying amazed.

Young children are models of amazement. They help us appreciate and celebrate the simple things in life. Last summer while sitting on the beach, I found my attention totally captured by a young boy playing at the edge of the water. For the longest time he picked up rocks, closely examined them, and tossed them one by one into the lake. He seemed to take great pleasure in the "plopping" noise audible as each rock pierced the water. Once the rock toss was over he began fashioning balls of sand, which he then set on the tip of his shovel and catapulted forward. Every time he tossed a sand ball over his shoulder, he quickly ran into the lake to see where it had landed. He looked completely amazed by how the sand dissipated once it hit the surface. The whole time he was playing he was singing to himself. My heart filled with joy watching this young boy communing with nature under the midday sun. Everything seemed delightful and new. He drew enjoyment from such simple things. As I prepared to leave the beach I asked myself at what point I had stopped being amazed, and had started taking things for granted. In my journal that afternoon I wrote: *Many lessons to be learned from this little boy. He has such joy within… he dances from the inside out.*

I encountered another joy-filled child while in a hospital elevator one day. A little girl was standing next to me tucked in behind her mother. Her body language led one to believe she was shy and reserved, but as the elevator door closed and began its ascent, she squealed "Weeeeeeee!" All of the adults in the elevator looked down at her and giggled. We joined in on "Weeeeeeee!" at the next floor when the elevator door opened and closed and we resumed our climb. As adults we had likely all entered the elevator that morning with heavy hearts born of concern for a sick loved one, yet in a matter of seconds this young girl made us smile, and reminded us of the need to stay amazed by life's simple things. How vital it is for the health of our soul that we play, enjoy life's simple pleasures, stay amazed, and be grateful for the many blessings in our lives...including the wisdom of little children.

In order to have an "attitude of gratitude" we must leave an opening for life to surprise us. We need to embrace mystery as a valued part of life and trust that grace flows from the unknown. This entails letting go of fear and of the need to make life as predictable as possible, moving ourselves instead to a place where we simply ponder and "be with" life. In order to do this we must trust that we are being led to where we are meant to be. For a number of years I worked alongside a fellow guidance counsellor, who in an attempt to alleviate graduating students' anxieties, would assure them that they would end up "where they were meant to be." Similarly, growing up I would often hear trusted adults tell me that "everything happens for a reason." I used to think such proclamations were simplistic and naïve, but the older I get and the more life I live, the more I find myself adopting these beliefs. I no longer view these statements as naïve at all, and in fact, now maintain that life does indeed unfold as is meant to. I am not referring to predestination, for I certainly believe that we play an active role in the shaping of our lives. I am simply suggesting that if we are open and discerning, we are led to the lessons we are intended to learn. I trust that there is purpose in everything; we are standing where we are in this particular moment in time for a precise reason. I am increasingly comfortable with uncertainty due to my belief that if we live consciously, what is true will find its way.

I wholly appreciate that when we are bogged down in the muck of life, it is extremely difficult to trust in uncertainty and the belief that "everything happens for a reason." When journeying through the loss of a loved one, for example, and finding ourselves in the early stages of grief, we quite rightly take little comfort in being asked to trust that "everything happens for a reason." In time we may come to believe this, but hearing such statements brings little consolation when we are fully immersed in our suffering. When caught in the depths of our pain it is hard to imagine any redemptive reason for its occurrence!

Someone once said, "When one door closes, another one opens... but they neglect to tell you it can be hell in the hallway!" How true! There is no denying that it can indeed be "hell in the hallway." It is always difficult to find ourselves standing in that in-between time, immersed so deeply in our pain that we cannot see the tunnel, let alone the light at the end of it! Yet, our lived experience shows us time and time again that if we are able to hang on and trust, a new door eventually opens and the sun breaks through once more. With time and reflection, we come to understand why it was we had to walk through the flames. Frequently, it is only in looking back that we are able to discern the reason for our suffering. It is then that we are extended an invitation to be transformed by our pain and become more tender to the touch.

Living through painful experiences humbles us. As our feelings of vulnerability move to the forefront we come to realize, perhaps for the first time in our lives, how profoundly we need each other. Humility fosters empathy and compassion, which positions us beside others, not above them. It is important, therefore, to be grateful not only for the blessings in our lives, but for our walks through the fire, which tenderize and deepen us.

Adopting an "attitude of gratitude," immersing ourselves in nature and the cycle of the seasons, and creating time to be silent and still are all powerful ways to nourish our soul. If we do not provide sustenance for our soul it will starve, and along with it our enthusiasm and passion for life. Then sadly, the world is deprived of the unique contribution we are called to make. Failing to feed our soul relegates us to the passenger seat, where someone or something (money, work, perfectionism, addiction, societal expectations....) is more than willing to drive our soul for us, moving us further from our essence and from who we are called to be.

Our soul is sacred, it is divine, it is eternal, and it is inspired. We need to work in rhythm with our soul by nurturing, protecting, and honouring it, so that we stay in the driver's seat — where we evolve in consciousness, expand in wisdom, grow in compassion, and reap the joys of *a deepening life*.

Life pounds at the seashore of my existence. It feels good to turn my back temporarily on everything and everyone, and just "be." How my soul has longed for this peace...the clear view of the water, the waves gently rolling into shore, like children tumbling down a hill. Such calm in the air, and such a calm in me too. I thank Sophia for these graced moments, and feel immense gratitude that I have found my way here today.

Deepening Your Life…

Who and what drives your soul?

In what specific ways do you feed your soul?

In what ways do you need to surrender and let go, and to grieve "what was" in your life?

Do you have a "sacred space" where you can go to let your soul breathe and speak? If yes, where? If no, what value might it add to your life to create one?

Are you able to sit still and be quiet within? If not, what do you think is causing your spirit to be restless? What steps might you take to enable yourself to just "be"?

What season are you currently experiencing in your inner life? Do you think it is possible to experience more than one season simultaneously?

For whom and for what are you most grateful? In what concrete way(s) do you express an "attitude of gratitude" in your life?

Why is it difficult for you to trust in uncertainty?

Have you had an experience of "hell in the hallway"? If yes, what did you do to get to the other side?

Do you believe that "everything happens for a reason" and that "we will end up where we are meant to be"?

What steps can you take to ensure you "Stay Amazed"?

EPILOGUE

It was on a winter afternoon five years ago, that I set a piece of chart paper on my dining room table, wrote on it *A Deepening Life*, turned on some instrumental music, lit a candle, and began inscribing what freely flowed from my soul… grace, tranquility, nature, waiting, surrender, struggle, compassion, wonderment, freedom, joy, desire, longing, stillness, emptiness, purpose, knowingness, pain, integrity, being, love, loss, hope, authenticity, courage, awe, wholeness, vulnerability… the page filled quickly. As I looked over the words, I realized that they captured the essence of my lived experience and I noticed certain themes emerging, which then became the focus of my chapters.

At the outset I had no idea how prophetic the title of my book would be and how much I would *deepen* in the process of writing my book. It was an incredibly rich experience to reflect over an extended period of time on the first half of my life. Spending significant amounts of time alone with my thoughts and feelings was a deepening experience in and of itself. The cyclical process of reflecting-writing-reflecting allowed me to pull together the threads of my lived experience and discern their tapestry of meaning.

Reflecting intensively on my life has expanded my spirit and grown my soul. It has helped me come to understand myself more deeply, and has enabled me to appreciate the fullness of my humanity in all its imperfection. Writing this book has facilitated my being gentler on myself, because as I reflected on the significant experiences of my life I came to see that in those times when I hurt others, it was not with any conscious intent to do so, but was the result of my own brokenness at the time. Coming to this realization has brought increased emotional and spiritual freedom.

As part of my pre-writing ritual I called upon *Sophia* and the spirit of my father to guide my writing. As I invoked them I lit a candle and placed it next to my laptop. The glass candleholder I housed the candle in holds deep meaning for me. It was used in a prayer celebration I wrote and presided over when my father died. The lit candle helped me stay connected to him throughout the writing process. Before his death I made him aware of my plan to write a book, and asked him if it would be okay if I dedicated it to him and my mother. He did not respond to my question initially so I assumed Alzheimer's had caused him to forget, but with time he looked over at me, and said with some hesitation, "I *think* that would be okay." His answer made me smile. He always liked to consider things carefully before committing, and his response was certainly humbling! On his deathbed I asked him to help me write my book when he was on "the other side." Undoubtedly he heard me because he and *Sophia* have been faithful writing companions! As I write these words today, a candle burns brightly in the candleholder on the table beside me.

At times I found it difficult to know what to include and what not to include, so I decided to trust in the creative process and in the movement of the Spirit. In doing so, there were surprises along the way. For example, I had no intention of writing about my grade seven teacher, Sister Perpetua, but as I typed the title *Guided by Grace*, she immediately came to mind. Thinking about her led me to reflect on my childhood years, which brought me to the realization of how significant a presence she was in my spiritual journey. It then became clear that she needed to be named as one of my *spirit guides*. I am sure Sister Perpetua never knew at the time what a strong impact she was having on me. I know I did not fully appreciate the extent of her influence until I set out to write this book.

Another surprise was how readily I found myself revisiting the same feelings I had felt when experiencing the life events I was writing about, even events that had occurred many years before! For example, when writing in chapter four about a relationship I had hoped would hold a future for me, I felt some of the same feelings of longing and sadness I felt originally when experiencing the loss. And in writing about coming out to my parents, I felt a trace of the same jitters I felt that Holy Thursday night, over twenty years ago, when I sat across from them at the kitchen table and shared the truth of who I was. I found it difficult to work on chapter one for extended periods of time, because it was emotionally draining to relive some of the memories connected to my father's debilitating disease and eventual death. I was surprised by how close to the surface my emotions were when reflecting on some of my lived experiences. I know it will be important for me to stay with these feelings, because they obviously have more to teach!

I spent much time reflecting on what picture I wanted to use for the cover, because I wanted to ensure the image adequately captured the content within. It was for this reason that the image I chose was that of my solo kayak. Not only have many of my most soulful and deepening moments occurred from the seat of a kayak, but the journey of the soul is ultimately an individual one. It is a solo journey where we are offered ongoing opportunities to learn and grow in consciousness, and it is up to us as individuals to say "yes" or "no" to these soulful invitations. In Jungian thought water symbolizes the unconscious, and I felt that its inclusion, alongside the kayak, helped capture the essence of what this book conveys — that a deepening life evolves from ongoing conscious dialogue with the events of our lives, which helps render the unconscious conscious and foster wisdom, which expands our soul and allows us to live more freely.

As I stated in the introduction, one of my intentions for writing this book is to assist others in deepening *their* lives, so they can grow in consciousness, share wisdom, and contribute to the expanding consciousness of the world. This was the rationale for including *Deepening Your Life* questions at the end of each chapter. These questions are intended not only to guide individual reflection but to support small-group sharing.

Everyone has a book living inside of them; some people just choose to write it down. I invite book clubs to form *Sophia (wisdom) circles* and reflect on the summary questions together. *Sophia circles* would create grace-filled opportunities for people to break open their "books," to share the wisdom of their life journeys. These circles would enable individuals to gather with others who share a commitment to growing in consciousness and staying awake for their lives!

Thank you for spending time with my words and thoughts. I hope something in my book has affirmed you, challenged you, provided insight, and deepened your life in some way. As you journey forward, trust your soul and the abiding presence of grace in your life. Gather the wisdom from your life's lessons and share the gift of your insights with others. Say "yes" to the soul's invitation to go deeper...you will not regret it.

What is a Deepening Life?

It is a life that marvels at itself as it unfolds.

It is a life lived mindfully: a life lived purposefully, with intent.

It is a life that is conscious and free, embedded in all that is true.

It is a life lived with unbridled openness to the wonder and mystery of everything, including darkness.

It is a life that honours and celebrates the divine within, and trusts that God is infused as much within as without.

It is a life forgiving of past mistakes and gentle towards regrets.

It is a promise to self that one's essence will never be compromised, for anything or anyone.

It is protecting and nurturing the place one has come to know within, and being a harbour for one's soul.

It is coming back home to self when feeling lost or abandoned.

It is taking time to experience and celebrate who a person is, rather than judge who they are not.

It is being a compassionate presence to the suffering of others — a wounded healer inviting others into a new day and a new way of being in the world.

It is embracing struggle and pain as the necessary heart-way to insight and an expanding soul.

It is standing in the darkness and trusting in the promise of light, when others have given up and gone home.

It is persevering on a difficult path when the easy road gets more adulation, acceptance, and support.

It is wisdom, hard earned, and in its own time.

It is trusting Sophia to lead us on…

References

Albums

Cockburn, Bruce. "Lovers in a Dangerous Time" *Stealing Fire*. Golden Mountain Music Corporation, 1984. LP.

Lights. "Drive My Soul" *The Listening*. Universal Music, 2009. LP.

Books

Canadian Conference of Catholic Bishops. *Catechism of the Catholic Church*. Ottawa: Concan Inc., 1992. Print.

The New Revised Standard Version Bible with Apocrypha. New York: Oxford University Press, 1989. Print.

Rich, Adrienne. *Of Women Born: Motherhood as Experience and Institution*. New York: W.W. Norton & Company, 1995. Print.

Rupp, Joyce. *Prayers to Sophia*. Philadelphia: Innisfree Press Inc.: 2000. Print.

ACKNOWLEDGEMENTS

I wish to thank my family for their unconditional love and support: my parents, Jean and Fred; my sisters: Suzanne, Ann, Cathy and Mary; my brothers-in-law: Kelly, Paul, Jim and Garth; my nieces: Danielle (and her husband Darren), Kristy (and her husband Joe) and Leah; my nephews: Brad, Sean, Adam, Noah, Jacob, Andrew, Alec and Emmett; my great nieces: Camryn, Emily, and Elle; and my great nephews: Ben and Nolan.

Sincere thanks to all my friends, who without fail supported me and respected the time I needed to hibernate and write so I could fulfill my dream of completing this book. Thank you so much for understanding how important this soulful project was to me, even if it meant less time joining you for biking, hiking, golfing, kayaking, cross-country skiing and enjoying "refreshments" on the deck in Southampton!

Immeasurable thanks to the critical readers who took time to carefully read and respond to my manuscript. Their insightful feedback enhanced and enriched my book: Patti Brannigan, Cathy Everrett, Mark Godin, Laurie Hanmer, Graham Jackson, Joanne McCabe, Sue Morrison, Joanne Regan, Shannon Rutherford and Kristi York.

Thank you to Marlene Keranen, photographer and friend, who took the photo for the back cover.

Thank you to lifetime friend, Bill Haber, who provided encouragement and sound advice flowing out of his own experience writing a book.

Thank you to BJ York, ally and friend, who helped a gay colleague stay somewhat sane while working in a closet!

Thank you to Cody, my loyal "fur person," who faithfully slept at my feet as I wrote the early chapters of this book. You are deeply missed. Until we go for walks together again...

Sincerest of thanks to the many LGBTQ students with whom I have journeyed these past thirty years. I am humbled and inspired by your courage and strength. Always believe in yourself, celebrate the divine within, and *never ever* apologize for being who you are!

Last, but certainly not least, thank you *Sophia,* for your guidance and abiding presence. You helped position my mind, heart, and soul so I could put thoughts into words and share my story of *a deepening life.*

To contact the author:
www.joangrundy.com

To order copies:
www.volumesdirect.com